About the Author

Always having been driven to explore the wonders of life and the mind, he has lived a quirky and solitary life, loving meditation, and connection to people and art– aspiring to his highest ideals, never giving way until his spirit is quenched. He is dedicated to producing the best, he possibly can and often chooses means that might seem too thorough. His life seems to be blooming in areas that he never thought possible all the time, and finding solutions that bring a greater passive joy into one's life is a motto of his - it makes life worth living in a subtle and innocent way.

Peaces

Ferdinand Jensen

Peaces

Olympia Publishers
London

www.olympiapublishers.com
OLYMPIA PAPERBACK EDITION

Copyright © Ferdinand Jensen 2024

The right of Ferdinand Jensen to be identified as author of
this work has been asserted in accordance with sections 77 and 78 of
the Copyright, Designs and Patents Act 1988.

All Rights Reserved

No reproduction, copy or transmission of this publication
may be made without written permission.
No paragraph of this publication may be reproduced,
copied or transmitted save with the written permission of the publisher,
or in accordance with the provisions
of the Copyright Act 1956 (as amended).

Any person who commits any unauthorised act in relation to
this publication may be liable to criminal
prosecution and civil claims for damage.

A CIP catalogue record for this title is
available from the British Library.

ISBN: 978-1-80074-706-7

This is a work of fiction.
Names, characters, places and incidents originate from the writer's
imagination. Any resemblance to actual persons, living or dead, is
purely coincidental.

First Published in 2024

Olympia Publishers
Tallis House
2 Tallis Street
London
EC4Y 0AB

Printed in Great Britain

Dedication

I dedicate this book to the upliftment of spirits in the most delicate way possible. To share a feeling of joy I have been living all the way through writing this book. To pay tribute to the unique beings we all are, and celebrate the true wonder of being special.

Acknowledgements

Thank you to my supportive family; I know my enthusiasm might be difficult to deal with at times and I am not always understood, but your perseverance means a tremendous amount to me. I cannot love you enough and I am so glad we still have so much time we can spend together.

Foreword

Having compiled an assortment of writing that is meant to stimulate your thinking, I hope that these pages yield you some mindfulness and fitting fulfilment of spare time. They have been chosen from pieces I have written over a large amount of time of years and I think they shall serve you. Ranging from theoretical subjects to day-to-day conundrums, there should be enough to provide you with food for thought and conversation.

I like to think of myself as someone that analyses his perception to conjure up the entertaining essences that make the world of my mind the way it is. These writings I share with the yearning for other souls to benefit from my adventures through my experiences.

I leave you to read of my perception, knowing that it is merely a view that has changed, will change and is forever evolving within me.

Please take these opinions as objectively as you can and know that it is one perspective among all that there are – the last thing I want to do is incite offense or controversy.

I have not studied writing, yet I love to share opinions and get close to what some might call debate on various subjects that breach onto the existential.

None of this work is based on specific other work and has merely been churned out through contemplation in meditation and daily routine, not following a train of thought until I am satisfied with an answer that I can work with in my daily life.

Forever I will continue on meandering and wandering in the thought and hope that my journey is worth something to the outside world – so please enjoy as much as possible.

A loving thanks to the artists I adore; TOOL, Chevelle, Deftones, Imogen Heap, Linkin Park, Chris Cornell and all the bands he has worked in, Alex & Allyson Grey and Robin Williams' legacy for their guidance. These masters of their craft have helped me when I needed it.

– FC Jensen

Introduction

Introducing 'Peaces' – a book that seeks to stimulate mindful thinking and give a sense of pondering to your life!

This is a collection of summaries that I have gathered over a period of ten years and will showcase a time in my life where I was very deep in thought.

Readers should feel as though this book complements their meditation practice and provides "food for 'thought'.

The narrative is to guide and promote the change from a negative situation into a positive outcome through thinking.

It tackles issues that might arise in day-to-day life where objective and broad thinking is needed to arrive at a more balanced and realistic notion of how complex life is, and how matters that we seem to not have control of can be simplified into a better and more rounded attitude.

Please be aware that this book serves as an example of how to think, and is by no means 'the' way of thinking or seeking to impose and archetype of thinking. It is wise to assume that this is just a perspective among the infinite ones we find in this existence.

Precautions

As a pre-emptive measure, I would like to warn you that you might often come across the terms 'Oneness', 'being one' and 'spiraling' when reading my work. These concepts are what I associate with a natural 'end' or goal toward only the individual understands, and works towards, and can be associated with "inner peace".

Oneness, for me, is a state one reaches that has you not just accepting the outer and inner world, but being okay with it to such a degree that you can carry on living in greater personal peace. It has an air of being versatile when tackling what life throws at you daily, by transcending what might upset you with good philosophy and ability, so that you lessen frustration and anger to the point where you sustain the 'attack'. It goes into understanding the fact that it is your own interpretation that is lacking when something breaks you down to such a degree that you become depressed or hopeless. Of course, this is not always the case – people can be cruel and unknowing of the damage they deal, but I think it is wise to know that you always have the power to cultivate your own reactions to happenings in your life, and can smooth things out so that the heart experiences a more even and balanced form of consistent energy.

'Being one' is a tricky one, for you cannot just decide 'I am the one', and then suddenly everything is fine. It's a dream of sorts that manifests a calmer, more harmonious self in which one experiences an ever-greater connection to the sea of life. . An increase in connection to all that we are together, along with nature and the rest of creation/existence. It becomes a feeling that I, for one, am addicted to. A kind of resonance with others and myself that I feel brings me joy and contentment with how everything is functioning and how I am being without any kind of deep necessity to change anything immediately, or even force anything into being. I suppose it is trusting in the universe and divine timing. A sense of knowing that things work out the way they should and all you are doing is the best you can.

Now, spiraling out has to do with the philosophy of ending things; seeing them through. Following the spiral until you've had enough and make a zig zag out of it, or reaching its center. I have found it valuable, even vital to see things through to point where it is like a math equation that you solve. There is a different energy to it when you finish things according to your own standards.

So there – I think there has been enough beating around the bush.

Let Me Be Your Guide

Being so bad at small talk, I'd rather show you or circumvent, a subject and then get to its core through words right away. The spirit is what I enjoy talking about and listening to people speak about their spiritual experiences gives me so much joy. It, however, is one of the most difficult things you can do, at times – speaking from the spirit or a hurt heart. It's a matter of connecting to that peaceful side of you that calms down all the current irritation and lends focus to being at rest in your soul.

If you are restless or in need of quiet, try taking smooth, soothing breaths and focusing your mind on reading these words as you take them in and let them resonate with you.

This is not some form of channeling that will miraculously make you feel better, but a request for your attention. I wish to connect you through this writing as if we were speaking to each other in a calm, respectful way. Resonating with phrases like 'I am', and 'namaste' will bring you to the center using the verbal form of calming down.

The 'I am' state is your basic state and connects you to the peace in the multiverse, or the 'all that is', etc. – there are few utterings that can mean the same, so please hold it dear. 'Namaste' means I recognize the divinity in you, whereby you recognize the divinity in another and yourself, for we are all one infinite being expressing itself in so many endless forms.

If you wish to, you can practice connecting to the writer or storyteller of any piece of writing and find that your mind weaves an extraordinary tale. Feel free to practice on my other writings for it will strengthen our bond, as a reader becomes more at peace with the writer the more he or she reads their work. Call it an experiment in trust. I believe it will improve my writing and what else I bring to the table, for experiences are telepathically or energetically shared across existence. Your impression will end up with me eventually or rapidly, through the butterfly effect, and will stimulate me to write in a more certain way or give rise to the topics I have not yet discovered.

My journey is an everyday one where I contemplate my life and life itself, exchanging opinions and perceptions; I find worth sharing and taking in what I perceive in a manner that holds all parties involved to the highest respect I can muster. . So, by journeying with me, you might find a friend in writing, a listener. That is all I ask, for change may come sooner or later, but regardless, that you listen means an entire world to me.

In closing, I wish you much initiative and courage to take on your spiritual journeys, and I wish that you may find peace in your endeavors so that you may grow every day and count your blessings. Namaste.

Open-mindedness

We have certain beliefs that are communally questioned, that we hold on to and that need clarification on common acceptance for them to be validated. They are in the back of your mind, sort of that always-ready-to-talk-about subject. This is an area of progress that you strive to complete or get clarification on, and although this is good for you, it might distract you from things that are buried inside you. Being open to new perspectives is healthy, but it takes a trained soul to argue in a manner that keeps your dignity intact and does not make you yield to new beliefs too easily, or be too stubborn to admit that another point might be better to adopt.

Currently, most people are pretty, open-minded and accepting of one another, as long as it 'doesn't mean they have to change who they are. A figment of reality that we cannot ignore, which accepts others for being themselves, happy about it and fully reliant on what they find –'– for people to be themselves is what we want, and it feels good to accept another for who they are. It's a big step towards union when one notices how things were – stereotypes were rampant, and categorization was constantly barring the progress of evolving yourself to be all you can be.

We live in a world where differences are celebrated and the common unity is discredited – minorities rule the world, and it's difficult to find unity in large groups.

The world is adjusting to the massive scope it's gotten, and needs time to really get its mind around the enormous amount of different beliefs that are so prevalent – trying to find the common denominator that connects us all together. As we find more and more common ground, the world will find a greater union – which is something we all strive for – a feeling of belonging to the community and feeling free within acceptance.

When everyone is similar it's easy to connect and feel 'one', but when there are so many specializations and niches it's difficult' to find your way. It might take some time to really relax into your being once you feel accepted by your peers, and more so the globe, for who you are.

Presently, there are few people that can't accept you for who you are on your public profiles and within your family and friends, so take a step forward and dare to express yourself that tiny bit more.

Free Will

This principle will most probably stay fascinating to everyone for long periods of time in their lives, for we are forever posed with how free we are.

What are manipulated actions and how much do our influences guide our wills into actions that may result in circumstances that we did not foresee, expect or want?

Furthermore, how much can we influence our vibes and behavior so that we are not massively at a detriment to the world in a way that barres us from true happiness as much as possible?

To me, the key lies in understanding. Having spent most of my days deep in thought about what my actual effect on the world is and how I can improve myself to be more 'in flow', I have found that the principle of doing good is good – for starters, doing bad with the intent of yielding a positive end result is the only way I can conscionably do bad... There must be bad I am doing that will always slip through the cracks of my awareness, and thereby is simply not under my control. The rabbit hole goes on!

Perception of what good and bad is has fundamental bases, yet some good and some bad is situational. It depends on view and dream, perspective, that guides into action so that (what I believe to be) the greater good is achieved.

Through mathematics, we know that the denominator must be the greater good, for we are all based on it. Yet, we all have our own roads to success – so this is what makes life so complicated.

We need structure and orders sometimes, but other times we need trust and creativity. Life is this balance between how much you can empower others without losing your own power/self-respect, and how good a complement you can be to the world.

Now, how much good are you, if you make a bad leader of yourself? Inherently, you will make bad decisions if you do not know yourself well enough to lead others. Also, how good is your vision when leading others? My point is that we need to find comfort within ourselves before we can go abroad. That's why there is such a big deal made of 'finding yourself'. It's important to know yourself as best as you can, for an improvement in society.

To take things into the dark side, I think there is a general sense of peer pressure in the world that bears down on all of us. So, we aren't solely in charge of what happens to us unless there is such a thing as complete awareness of oneself. This means the world's forces sometimes break, beings into states that incur the rest of the world harm and chaos. Not to mention the unnoticed mistakes that integral parts of society make due to innately not being capable of plugging every single hole there is.

The entire scenario becomes even more complex when introducing walls like blame or hatred along with commonly-accepted behavior like setting goals too high, or just believing in realities that are unconsciously the stuff of dreams, or not immediate possibility.

You see that this topic can go on and on, and I love that it does because it yields so much, which makes life so full of possibilities. The barriers are only in perception and this makes us free to be the artists of life. There is no measure of love you can give, yet how much do you give until it backfires? There are limits to reality – mostly set by principles, drive and dreams. The point I'm getting to is that, to me, it seems that experience is what matters most. It puts things into a manageable frame where the good and the bad can be appreciated no matter what your values.

I could go on, yet I think I've babbled enough on this subject – so there it is: my gist of it!

Acceptance

Being fine with yourself can be something you are used to; a negative behavior – yes, 'I'm fine with my flaws and positives, and as long as they balance each other out 'there's no reason to change. The crux of the matter is whether or not you truly accept yourself for who you are, and chances are if 'you've got work that needs to be done on the spirit, you 'don't know who the true you really are. At least, 'you're not in touch with your higher self.

Day by day, there are little things you say to yourself, call them compulsive behaviors, that fit into the self-image and don't bother you really if your ego is fine, but let's say your life is not going the way you planned, and that last failure is really nipping at your heels – your self-image suffers, and most of the time it's unrealistic. Either it's what you think the common perception of you is – a stereotype – or it's a degrading term meant to change your ways. Of course, there are also the general bullying terms used on many occasions which are typical of depression or being forced into a mental corner.

It can easily become a habit to get the bad voices inside you to shut up by giving them what they want, but that's never where it ends. Your conscience will be clear once you confront the reasons you feel inadequate and contemplate solutions – building a strong self-image takes time and patience, and most of all compassion. Be wary of making excuses or blaming others – these simply avoid the subject and provide a sense of failing to achieve the desired state of being.

Learning to accept others for how they are is also very challenging – the mind works in 'its own way, but depending on the information, experience and logic in it, people act differently, react differently, understand differently and generally have a different perspective. Each person has their own perspective and it's great that way – without this diversity, the world would come to a standstill. There are books on temperaments and studies on astrology describing how different people are and how they work together, and a further look into this might benefit you if you're into really figuring out how people tick – but for the most part it's vital to understand and accept that people change slowly in an unnoticed way, but never really change who they are on a soul level.

Things we cannot change put a damper on acceptance. Many facts in life need to be accepted for how they, are and once this is done, consistently maneuvering around and wielding the circumstances becomes easier. A healthy mind knows its surroundings well along with its capabilities, and pursues its goals in a calm and collected manner – no need to get out of tune.

By practicing acceptance you come to terms with yourself and your limitations and find out that that's okay – healthy barriers make you feel safe, and pushing your capabilities once you feel the need to arises really works wonders for confidence.

Comfort

I don't know about you, but from where I'm sitting, I'm very comfortable, and if you're reading this with any interest, you must be too.

Its rather easy to make a reasonable living – 'we're all slaves in some great monopoly's view, but at least 'we're comfortable slaves – the term loses its meaning, and 'we're just left with that nuisance of it being a fact in some capitalist's head.

Entertainment is what we live for along with the odd thrill to keep things interesting. So, comfort has become rather prevalent. Most people can afford it and need it. I have relatives that live comfortably but work all the time, but affording luxurious travels that also relax them, and I'm sure the homeless person under the bridge close by, also loves his beers until he drops into a relaxing doze.

Point is, we're adaptable; we choose a lifestyle and get comfortable with it – suiting our outside to our inside, and I really think everyone is where they need to be – comparison is a judging task once you take that step too far. So, as long as you compare to prove a point, I suppose it's safe, but looking down on one and raising the other somehow makes me think of the grey area – sneaky and mischievous.

Rest is what this world needs for the pressure we're under from bosses that want higher rewards and more work hours, and to do that" we need comfort. Who can relax on a wooden bench for extended periods of time – just the hobo that has the mad skills.

Comfort is something we gladly pay for – it's quality of life. Of course, You don't think spiritually unless everything in your life sort of works out well – so it's a luxury we can't afford often enough.".

[advised to explore the idea of part time.

Meandering

Being a part of my life, I find myself in this state quite often – the act of making sense of things, while sort of feeling as though I am procrastinating or being distracted.

It has a somewhat confused taint to it, but something within me tells me I need to go through it until I live with a greater clarity on subjects.

Seemingly aimless I feel at times, yet I have grown up with a lot of this in my life. There are so many areas that invoke this type of state in me that partially I sense that I have always been meandering into certain directions.

Now and then, unnoticeably, I realize that the amount of pressure I experience when doing this lessens.

Innately, I think we all meander at times, and sadly this act most probably is likened to stupidity or confusion.

It's not as deep as those two, and has something magical to it. It is a softer way of expressing the process of solidifying perception along with attitude – lending you more leeway to feel comfortable in this nearly unnerving state that culminates in greater self-confidence once you're out of it.

Meandering conjures up images of fog around dim light on a marsh in me sometimes, and when I feel better it's a meadow shone onto by a great floodlight. I get the sense of being in twilight, or that beautiful time before the proper sunrise.

Energies are gathering in preparation for something greater. Doing the necessary work that is swept under the rug once it can be named dawn confidently. Likening it to seasons, I imagine it to be the ending of winter or to tasks to, I imagine this to be like awaiting spring – it would be the middle, before one gets giddy from seeing the end in further sight.

The topic also reminds me of the boredom I feel when I am prone to wasting time on not having to meander all too much, as to bide time for when the entire act is more rewarding - procrastination. Unfortunately, there is a lack of motivation when we cannot be so hopeful of the future, sort of just going along until circumstances improve. Awareness of being in this period, I think, offers a lot of possibility for constructive reflection – a space in which one can truly work on foundations and other details that often slip through the cracks.

All in all, I like meandering, but it falls into a drawer in my consciousness that has a big lack of excitement. It's difficult for me to be jovial when I'm feeling as though I am between nowhere and somewhere – not really knowledgeable of how to get those bearings.

Nonetheless – I have gained a better understanding of being content in such times. Also, I have gained a knowing or wisdom of being certain that everything is at its right place always, even in slow moments toward goals and accomplishments.

Finally, being able to put my finger on it better – now I will no longer discredit this movement so much.

Wondering

This act is close to my heart because it has so much to do with imagination – too much of it leaves me blue-eyed and living in the illusion that is often scintillating to live through, but yields the offbeat disillusionment that sometimes breaches into disappointment.

Be that as it may, it's a hard pill you swallow at the start of your life. We cannot always get what we want!

Clinging to the wondering in life is part of us– almost like the cliff hangers we experience, it invigorates and stimulates – a feeling which, at its apex, is a bursting of joy. . An endless passtime activity that we yearn for in everything we live.

Just wandering in wondering…

Like a never-ending spiral, we are drawn to light like moths to a flame – artists keeping things interesting and new. I will never stop this activity, for I find it to be a spice of life – seemingly always drinking from the honey that is at the fringe of reality and expression. This beautiful void is so bottomless that I find myself forever falling within. Creative, I want to be – spreading wings, splashing in pools on the sides, and jumping on floating rocks and dancing across brides between mid-air islands.

At least my mind can't help itself – I do know, however, that there is safety and comfort in the knowledge of what is what and so forth… Yet, when compared to the sheer elation that comes and goes, I do feel more alive in this free space.

Not proficient at it yet, I do, however, have softer landings than I used to. Lots of motivating encouragement from the world has made me trust it in a greater way – giving myself the opportunity to get more comfortable in my own skin.

The word 'wondering' in itself has the quality of a wonder – so it's like a small thing one can do for oneself to appreciate all of it that there is in the world. Long gone is the intense fear of this space we live in – it's been put on the backburner so that it may melt into a calculated knowing of the dangers – instead of the opening of gates to them. It's a spark that opens up the mind into a better way of being – of course, this is merely a subcategory of bliss, yet I think it healthy to take small sips for personal pleasure.

We all want this in our lives, but who would have thought that this basic behavior could bloom into a thing so joyous when cultivated regularly – another gift you can give yourself.

Almost effortlessly we find ourselves in this state at times, unaware of the potential it has to brighten our days. Too seldomly do I delve so deeply, but it feels right for now.

Somehow, I have become disillusioned with a new and positive twist. I just hope I do not pay too high a price once my wondering goes back to wandering.

Bad Recipes

Having recently realized that I have specific recipes for happiness that are rigid in nature, I seek to loosen them. We build these energetic pathways that give us good feelings and we follow those and want to find people or things to fit the bill. It wasn't that extreme for me in comparison to what I've had to deal with. I have come across people whose bill I really didn't fit, and have felt outside of the norm a lot.

These 'bad recipes' seek to conform the world to your view, and cultivate frustration along with anger and disappointment. It's up to us to flow with the world, taking what we get or making the best out of what that is.

To be a leader does not mean holding a bad belief and making it real – making the world conform to a rigid desire. We have been molded into thinking that's a good thing, and that you need to stand your ground even if you get angry, but I find that to be a very juvenile way of handling life.

Having gone through many difficulties, I have learnt that some of my most rigid beliefs have been broken down again and again until I had a rounded view. You either weather the storm by being strong, or you bend with the wind. Life is more like flowing water and, depending on your view, can be more rapid or just a trickle when you're really still. The mind associates automatically and you can align accordingly.

If you're stubborn in your beliefs, you might associate with the big tree in the storm, but if that tree is an angry tree, it might just be more of a burning bush. Being strong means that you have a heart that is wise with compassion, and I've noticed that if you have little spiritual experience or have not healed a lot in your life, it's very difficult to find that compassion for others that are in tough spots.

It comes down to whether you're stuck in a 'fighting off' mentality, or an 'understanding and sharing your own perspective' mentality. You have many aspects to yourself, and some might be fighting off attackers while others might be welcoming like-minded reinforcements, but it's the peaceful that heal the sick back home that are at peace.

The points of view are vastly different – the fighters feel like warriors, which is the commonly accepted viewpoint that there are enemies, but the healers instead understand that we are all one, and that the best they can do is heal the ones that were wounded. The metaphor goes on to see the world as more of a spiritual growth school where we learn through smaller, painful experiences like rejection and misunderstanding.

Finding ways to communicate with the other side or sides is the way of the priest, that, in modern times, has become too righteous, in my opinion, becoming too specialized instead of accepting and open-minded. In the past, we were less fragmented into our cultures and the languages we speak; I hope we can translate beliefs so that we accept that there are so many that live together – furthermore, that the symbols are seen as not so realistic but more as manifestations of the mind that embody a certain trait.

It's like our messiahs have become these idols that no longer stand for what they believe in but for their religion. As though they are these physical beings that are nothing besides physicality and propaganda instead of their values.

When making new friends, for example, a 'bad recipe' would be to insist on them having to be atheist; it implies that they need to be against religion when there is always something that you can connect on, and that's the real 'belief'. Most religions preach togetherness and oneness, at least within their belief system. I believe that we are all trying to realize the same truth, and that is that there is no limit to consciousness.

Recently having realized that the law of one is so real that it is more understanding than factual, has made me very relieved that I don't have to <u>BELIEVE</u> in some kind of thing that might not be true, or have faith. So, I think that has definite value when you can understand something factually without having to go on what research you have done or what you've heard from others. This theme also resonates with the precipitate that is the 'greater good for all' mentality. It's so basic that it becomes a general cornerstone of being.

Few philosophical mantras have helped me as much as 'the greater for all', and 'we are all one'.

Bleeding Blossoms

On the far horizon, the sun goes down with a red glow; the moon is soon to be seen hanging in a black sky along with the white stars. The grey walkway is skirted with brush that shines maroon. On each side, in the distance, trees create a black rim that makes it seem gloomy on this journey.

A lonely, white tree is the only being that catches the eye alongside this path. It has red blossoms that make it seem like it's bleeding. Here and there I find a blossom on the ground.

This entire scenery speaks of a philosophical and clean spirit that suffers on the inside for its good deeds it does for the greater good of all. Each of us share the consciousness and contribute to the general health of the overall mind. Quantum physics suggests that we are all examples of the whole in small form; even in nature we find that the overall pattern reflects in smaller form over and over the more one zooms in.

So, theoretically all we do matters – even the smallest thing. Our suffering is communal, yet what is yielded from suffering is often elation. At its end, one always conquers suffering.

The suffering tree so internally conquers suffering and bleeds out beauty onto the road that it is dark yet lit by the fading sun, and the glimmers of hope that are the moon and the stars.

I find that this scenario depicts reality in a melancholic light, with so much truth at its core even though the painting is rather dark.

We usually see ourselves as the white tree, because none of

us think that we are bad at our core. We are the product of our choices and what life gives us, so in a sense we are transmuting life as best we can. Always being bright at our core and having to deal with amounts of darkness and light. Some come into life blessed, and others have a difficult life, yet we all make it an even burden to bear.

We get used to conditions, regardless of how bad or good, and we find the mean between ease and difficulty so that we all suffer and live off the elation.

In my view, life is so filled with the mundane that I am used to my attention falling sometimes on the good and sometimes on the bad. It fluctuates with influences I get through going with the flow of my general, mood and by fighting the negative current. It's like there is an invisible force I call 'involuntary depression' that is present all the time. It lessens sometimes and increases at others, we can but combat it by living on and weighing the storm. Human beings among all mammals are the only ones that need reason to live, or else we kill ourselves. So, is it too much to claim that we struggle with contentment on a cultural scale?

We have practices in place that teach us to live and let go because we are so used to the abnormal in our rampant times that we cannot adhere to the laws of nature and find understanding that is not somehow unnatural.

We find things to believe in that make us wonder about life beyond this one, neglecting what we do every day to make life good long-term. For now, we are a forest of trees that all bleed their color blossoms all over the paths that cut through it. All of us sharing by making the grey road colorful in the evening.

Circumvention/Evasion

This topic is one of my favorites, because it revolves around quirkily, sneakily and creatively beating around the bush before you set it on fire.

The art of a good conversation is longevity and the sense of youth of the subject.

We easily fall into habits of not uncovering the mystery within what is being said – so one of my tactics is to become aware of the majesty in an act of tapping into the wonder.

It makes conversing fun by sidestepping the obviously implied too harshly, tuning into that awakening energy and then finding a way of tailoring one's next words with such detail, yet in the spirit of a gentle touch so that they might meet their mark.

It is a subtlety that is precarious at times in our determined world – for we must sidestep the old, used and downtrodden narratives in the subtext to shed light on a new way of seeing things with our eyes open.

Evading contradiction and too extreme stances yield a feeling of personal security in one's opinion – not having to defend immediately as one is too used to in ultimatum scenarios.

The question is: how long can you last not having to face direct evidence that seems to be irrefutable within the confines of the partaker in the conversation?

There are many techniques one can adopt – much of which deal with the strategy of making things safe to deliver the final argument in a harmless way.

It has a sense of birthing an idea that will hold. Working on a good base before gently opening the door to a realization instead of defeat or victory.

We are so accustomed to a win/lose stage that we forget that there is only one coin.

Long gone are the days of black and white – this is outmoded, in my opinion. Holistic perception deals with seeing AND believing. This requires proof and understanding.

So, who would enter a debate that he is not ready for? Overzealous and greedy individuals that seek an end instead of new beginnings will surely not do well in a field of rounded, optimistic yet not blue-eyed and diplomatic perceptions.

We can only share our perspective, that is what we have to work with. . So why aren't we being humble and sharing recyclable opinions instead of hard and chiseled facts?

Don't Block Your Light

This is something that I do so often; I discredit myself and my observations about myself. Even though I am an eccentric when it comes to opinion, I have struggled with keeping people entertained by my notions. Thriving on the wonder that is conversation, my view seems to not grip the imagination of the many, which makes me so grateful that you're reading this. It brings me such joy that someone would take a few minutes out of their life to appreciate something that is not in the 'ordinary'.

Your attention makes a difference to me, entertaining you and maybe teaching you something along the line or just being any other kind of virtue to you is at the core of my joy. So, attempt to convey your heart in everything you do, choose those that would appreciate it and share mindfully in the high spirit that would serve them. We need to measure how much we can give – I have trouble with always giving too much and then being disappointed with not getting equal in return. But I believe that it all balances out.

We easily get hurt if we follow a certain measure; we derive ourselves, but let the universe balance that for you – it's a very subconscious feeling that lets you know that you will get what you deserve. This often makes me nervous and koi, for I am used to going full out – so people go out of their way to stem me. They cannot take someone so bold the same way I cannot take someone that is so overly repressed. So, I try to find the spark, trying to let them know through too much love that there is someone that is interested.

Not blocking your light means that you do not stand in your own way, so I have calmed down and learnt to measure what I share, and also adopting my bad attempt at small talk. The point is to connect to yourself and share that, often with yourself first before you can openly share it with others. It takes a journey to know the different parts of yourself – this does not mean to create an ego that you then explore, but to find patterns in your being and adjust appropriately.

Mostly it takes long to even begin being interested in the self, but as others show interest and you feel that you might be a benefit to yourself and them, you get on your feet.

It seems like no big thing being interested in another or yourself due to the sheer numbers we are – what is another person in this massive world full of perceptions? But, I tell you it does matter. Remember I have spoken about how you are the ocean in a drop, in this way your joy is felt by the world and the people you speak to or engage with. So, every experience you go through matters!

It takes a massive amount of time and is not worthwhile to sit down and try to find out all the good things about you before you enter the world – the world helps you recognize those things along the way. You may grow with everyone around you as we all endlessly delve into ourselves and each other's consciousnesses – it's an endless celebration discovering the self.

So, put on your happy pants and get walking or jump for joy, because there is no limit to your happiness.

For those that are too realistic – smirk at the notion of doing something like this in secret (the jumping is something I never do – just in my mind).

Expanding

This week I have let go of my incessant attention to detail when it comes to my thinking. I got overwhelmed by analyzing everything so intently and getting lost in the nuances of specific energies and emotions along with thought paths. It has been relieving, exciting and daunting to open my mind up to a broader perspective that affords me more peace and tranquility.

It's as though air has rushed in and made me calmer, I must say, though, that the process of letting go was not an easy one. Having struggled with repeating thoughts that weigh on my heart, it was like stopping a siege machine that was relentless and ever so resilient. It was a conglomerate of thoughts that tied into one another, forming bands of energy that kept me locked in place. Escaping was a matter of summoning all my reserve energy to take those final steps.

As I made headway, I slowly felt the tear away from distorted energy, and I was greeted with the realizations of what life was like under those vibes and how different it is over here.

Feeling not much different in my core self but being released from such horrid vibrations, I came to know what it's like moving into a new field of awareness. Having learnt from the old, it's my way of progressing to gain realization instead of merely noticing a trend. The knowledge I gained was permanent, and I will never forget it. I certainly won't be playing around with vibes and thoughts in my mind again, and will treasure the expanding into the new that I am experiencing now.

It's a matter of dividing what does not serve you with such tenacity that you cut every tie. It had a serious addiction aspect to it, for I would always lose hope and fall into a lower state of thought and restart the cycle that would inevitably be bested again and again until there was nothing left to hold on to. Constantly transmuting the negative with new kinds of positive that might work so that one does not get immune to the same positive.

It was like conquering myself, for I had vested interest in keeping the negative in place. It's like a comfort zone that cells in your body have adapted to and fight for, that can only be convinced with definite proof that the other side is better.

Things like 'the grass is green on both sides of the fence' come to mind. No matter where you are there are always problems, but what matters is which kind of problems you want to have. Having gotten tired of the old, I never felt like I belonged and was constantly walking on eggshells, completely out of place and specialized in my small awareness.

I feel better now, more at home and capable of expanding into my fuller self – I don't know how far I want to go, because my last trip down the rabbit hole had me heaving philosophical boulders all day long. I want to calm down and get in touch with my serious side.

I have a side to me that is very detached and is seen as unaware of the seriousness in life whereas I see the world as too serious and get overwhelmed, which triggers a lightheartedness that I cannot substantiate. *Just see the lighter side of things and life's not so bad* is my motto, but it has led me astray. This world is not friendly in the sense that it's easy to handle – every day one is faced with having to deal with issues that the world has, and it gets me down.

It's gotten to a point where I'm numb to it, but affected anew – deepening the hole of numbness, which makes me retreat to the world of the mind where everything functions.

At least I can organize and figure out problems here where there is no criticism and pressure. When my mind is under attack, I can sort it out and the problem goes away – the outside world does not seem like that. We have issues that persist like my delusion that would not go away, and they confront us. There is always the call to become aware and solve what is ailing us – I just don't feel like I'm the person who's to call.

People that can solve problems for the rest are engaged in solving them while there is a group invested in the opposite – it's a big movement that is slow and painful. It's like torture. But know that once it's over, you are free to unwind and ease your consciousness.

Fitting In

I have recently been broken by my need to fit myself into something I'm just not. Just always wanting to grow, I set myself the goal to be more aware of my place in the world, so I endeavored to try things I'm not good at and to learn them. I know myself better now, and I'm developing a feel for what I will excel at to get back into my natural rhythm. It feels bad to force yourself into situations that are bad for you and forces you to grow in ways that are very uncomfortable.

Naturally you have a knack for where you want to go and what you want to do with your life, and mine has been, for the most part, to expand upon my faults and rid them of my life. One of these faults was the insecurity I felt about what I was good at. Having felt that I was so good at it that it was like play to me, I didn't think people owed me anything in return because I was having so much fun with it, but now I'm suffering the hard reality of not being independent. It's difficult when you don't even take your own profession seriously enough to make a living off of it. So how will potential customers invest in you?

Another aspect of my learning was to connect to people that aren't as deep as I am. This was a massive pitfall for me. Only now am I connecting to people that really matter to me, whose opinions I cherish and want to listen to. I have thrown my happy-go-lucky view down the toilet and gotten a walking-on-eggshells attitude that I find appalling. Constantly being awkward and not knowing what to say to the other person because you don't feel at harmony with yourself is a terrible prison.

It has given me immense drive to reconnect to my truest self so I can be calm, connected and comfortable in my skin. I really don't want to spend another second feeling out of place.

The third mission I gave myself was improving my listening skills and awareness. I would be distracted in conversation and push my motives so that they force someone into a corner at times when I needed to get my point across. I went through some miscellaneous bad behaviors, and have since really worked on listening better, aligning my intentions to delivering a helpful response, and prolonging the conversation so that it goes full circle.

I treated life as a game and manipulated myself to learn from it as much as I could at a dire cost. Luckily, I feel as though I'm at the end of this journey where I can be honest about it and share my findings in a sort of confession to the universe. I hurt people along the way and got hurt back and it's been a daunting time that I will never forget – that which I learnt is irreplaceable and I wouldn't trade it for the world, but I am truly tired, spiritually.

I have never done such a massive amount of spiritual work in one go before; the need to reach harmony was so intense that I spent weeks and years on it. Finally, I feel as though the fog has lifted and I can relax and unwind into myself. I am going to go through some discomfort aligning back to true ways as I have to shed what does not serve me, but at least the rest of what I have to do is mostly energetic and not mental. Gone are the days of suffering in delusion and disconnection, and here come the days of honest, humbleness, connection and harmony.

Having my internal energies align with my dreams is finally a reality. Before I was lost in infatuation, always chasing the dopamine rush you get from starting something new but not being able to follow through due to lack of true commitment. It comes when you can align your dreams, thoughts and stance with going through the entire process, kind of unconsciously putting your eggs into that basket. It feels good to be working on something that has longevity and does not feel like a passing fad or a pipedream.

I used to be addicted to quick results and easy fixes, but I feel as though I'm changing into someone that likes the long haul again. It was like a roller coaster ride, always something new. Nowadays I find visiting the older and trusted ways is relieving, and they get updated by the new to make them fresh again.

Having learnt a lot, I will be integrating all this yummy knowledge to form a proper balanced me that is a blend of my good old habits and the wisdom I have gained through going through my training.

In case you ever choose to endeavor in things like these that I have spoken of, then know that it is not for the faint of heart and it will break you along the way. There are few things that balance a person as much as recovering from being broken, so rather take smaller steps than I and bend like grass in the wind ever so often – it's far more efficient and so much easier on your soul.

Glimpse of my Spiritual State

Always having the need to share what I come across, I feel like circumventing a subject being at greater peace than before. Ever wanting to display my journey, I wish to give testimony as to there being such a thing as awakening spiritually and that there is such a thing as progress. Many souls I feel are locked into a risk-and-reward system that has them attempting to do the spiritual work but not seeing immediate results, and then letting it go with no respect or regard for the changing procedure.

It takes a measure of starting anew in one's life and letting go of past convictions, not to a new sense of having failed but to a sense of morphing into something even greater. You might feel as though your past self is finished and that it's time to start fresh with confidence. You might feel like a newborn at first, but get yourself a hug from someone that appreciates you for who you are always, like your mother or father.

I recently got over a giant block in my consciousness that I had been carrying with me nearly all my life – I had felt fragile and immediately went to get the remedy. Sometimes you know what you need as if it's instinctive, and other times it seems like that thing you cannot grasp just yet. Work on in your effort to attain and manifest this dream in your life – always listening to your true, subtle and gentle inner self for guidance.

In my life it has become the main focus to evolve spiritually, and I enjoy it sometimes a little too much – my professional life suffers, and I make slow and precarious progress in it. It's not alarming to me, and I do my best to keep away from pressure-filled thought so that I may be close to my higher self. It is not easy for me to deal with the reality I am faced with, as even smaller things become giant sometimes as I make mosquitos elephants, but I return to a calm self and know that I will conquer every obstacle. For life never poses us with what we cannot truly handle.

This overwhelming truth often tries to break me down as I make living up to it so incredibly important that my knees buckle, but there is knowing and trust in my ability.

Continually, I hope you can relate to what I have to say, and I attempt to shy away from repeating myself, even though some things I find really need to be rehashed to sink in fully – repetition of comforting knowledge often helps me conquer small and big issues in my life. As I move closer to achieving the next step into my new self, I find that I have done this many time and am ready not to reinvent myself, but to add to an existing perception that I love building on.

When I was you, I got appalled at my ego and got rid of it, leaving me with a hole inside that I was so proud of, but now I am slowly rebuilding my ego to a balanced state where it can harmonize with the rest of me that has become so selfless. It is difficult for me to be so honest sometimes, in retrospect, and I feel somewhat ashamed of judging myself so highly when the way I've grown up has taught me to put myself second and the outside world first so that it may return in kind. But the world is not kind in that way here.

You need to out yourself first on the same level as the outside world and start giving fully so that you may receive fully – this is the bargain you may enter into, yet so many choose to trade along mental gradients in agreements that benefit the worship of the physical. I however, believe in a spiritual trade in which everyone wins and the world eventually lives in greater harmony.

My analysis of self must stop here for one can only take so much spiritual work at a time. Do not be gluttonous, I need to tell myself, for my hunger to improve my spirit is always there and I feel like I never get enough work done, which is my way of complementing the spiritual journey.

Healing Time

The way I foresee the coming time will be one of constant healing – we have moved into a new world that we need to really get used to. It will take some healing and readjusting to the new vibration until it enters our foundation.

I want to take this opportunity to mention some of my favorite artists; Alex Grey and the members of the bands *TOOL* and *A Perfect Circle*. Through my journey of awakening, I have long relied on their influence to guide me. Often, I have felt alone in my ways and needed the comfort of like-minded individuals that I know have made an example of what I call 'proper belief' in the multiverse. Their art revolves around the evolution of the consciousness as mine does, and they help people like me to realize their personal and impersonal dreams in this realm of the 'new'.

In one of their newer songs, TOOL displays the lyrics, 'control your delusion,' which always rings so true and reminds me of what we have to do now. We are in the cycle of letting go of the old, which includes letting go of the monetary system in the long run to no longer have monopolies reign in our global lives, such as governments that, regardless of what model they assume, take control of the resources and use it on themselves and their closed agendas.

We also need to work on improving the general state of interaction that we engage in in our daily lives. As our moods rise, every interaction will become more meaningful and it will become vital to take your place in the overall – not taking a lower stance but most of all not assuming a higher stance than what you are placed in. There are many that assume stances that place them above others in such a fashion that implies that they are 'better' than them, and then treat people accordingly – this is old behavior that needs to be gotten rid of, because in the new paradigm we align to our spiritual level, where your experience, growth and wisdom has the higher level of respect.

Therapy will be needed for the entire globe, so if you feel as though you could contribute or benefit from talking about your spiritual path, then open yourself up to digging deep and sharing what you have experienced and feel is at the forefront of your consciousness. It's about talking your head out so that you can finally connect to the heart, and eventually speak from there so that we in the end have a culture that can freely speak from the heart.

In a perfect circle song, they sing about not having time for chit-chat, and to 'get the lead out' – this is so fitting for what we have to do. We no longer have time to waste on just awkward elevator talk so that we can pass time – we really need to 'get the lead out'. We are carrying baggage with us that is unresolved and we make excuses to not take care of it. Sadly, and jubilantly at the same time, we have the opportunity to move through these burdens and cleanse our souls of the old – whatever that may be. For many it would be terrifying memories, losses and internal disagreements that torture us daily.

Our issues with what the world look like and how interaction is such a problem, changing so much from person to person that we don't have the freedom to speak openly about ourselves and share this safely with anyone, is a huge problem that will change in the future. We are on a long road to getting everyone on the same page regarding reality.

Our different beliefs pose the biggest problems but keeping those for yourself and honing them in solitude would be advisable. Really analyzing them in private sessions and making them applicable to daily life is key, for we have grown up in these fashions and can't shed any belief so easily. Recently I have been made aware of a very comforting perspective that made things easier for me; a friend mentioned that this guy I know is very religious but doesn't talk about it because it's his. Fear regarding belief is one of the many things that divide us, and this way of looking at it gives freedom to practice the belief in privacy where you can then go as wild with it as you please without having to convince others of your convictions, and don't have to suffer the fear of rejection. For even with my closest friends, I have a different view on, say, 'God', and it always becomes some sort of debate or discussion on what the best view could possibly be.

We function properly when putting our beliefs aside, and most of them are food for thought over many a year or lifetime, so talking about it just irritates and is beside the point regarding unity and togetherness. We don't need unnecessary fights over something that is so intangible that we cannot put words to it. I like boiling down to the 'words fail' argument, for it's something of little importance and will probably never be solved besides accepting the practice of looking inward for the answers instead of outward.

Another thing I would like to mention quickly is the presence or arrival of extra-terrestrials – they're not going to land and sort our problems for us. If they're here already, they're doing their part in helping us evolve so that eventually there can be contact. Should there be contact in the future it would be like talking to a messiah that would catapult the contactor into a state of figuring out what he or she needs to do to evolve for the dimensional difference is too high – if anything, we could only evolve into states that would balance our energies so that contact can even take place, and then there's the cultural difference to get over. It's just far more complex than some messiah landing in a UFO and telling us what we know already. We need to build a resource-based economy, heal the planet, and manifest the new vibrations into our foundations, and on top of that get used to them and live like that for so many years to come before even thinking of something like disclosure can happen.

There are too many blue-eyed individuals thinking that there's a quick fix for our problems – it takes mountains of time to cultivate a functional civilization from the ashes we are now in. At a glance we might seem okay, but this disconnected consciousness needs so much healing even though it's just broken the surface and is exhausted of that massive feat. The good news, though, is that it gets much easier. We gain velocity although we have lost our trust in the physical universe we know all too well.

Focus on the spiritual and what it yields in our daily lives is far more precious than anything we can achieve physically – for you keep the spiritual forever and build, morph and transform it as this investment that always serves you. Sharing your knowledge becomes of greater importance, and the more you gain the more you can share in a karmic practice that has everyone prospering from spreading the good. It will become this addiction to doing good in small acts all the time. This culminates in a healthy spirit that lends inspiration and courage to those in need. Creativity rises, and what you can do with your now-moment becomes this giant expanse where everything is possible in a realistic and appropriate fashion. The combination of great minds yields fun and excitement to produce great results for the spirit and the overall consciousness, for every experience is shared, regardless of how true it is or not – so, the more heartfelt your experiences are the more impetus they will have on the ones around you and the world at large. Collectively rising into a new vibration slowly heightens the average mood, and sooner or later has everyone involved in living in harmony.

Share what you need to feel more at peace with yourself and move on into a greater sense of self-acceptance as you journey into your spirit. Trust that it will become a regular thing that feels good to do.

Together, in our many factions, we rise to great levels.

In the Meantime

For the moment, I feel elated and jovial, for good news has brought hope into my life. The horizon is that tad brighter and the past is no longer as dim as before. My thoughts do not seem to dwell on the inevitable or fantastic and life seems a little more tangible.

Doing things that brighten my day do not seem so taxing today, so here and there I will engage in some activity where I can ignore the downsides for today.

Seemingly freed from the black and white for a moment in time, I have stepped into the colorful side of life – I do not know how long I will stay here, for euphoria mostly lasts only for a few hours, but I hope a derivative stay with me.

I wish to add to my foundation from this day and carry with me the glint in my eye. Life does not give gifts so often, so let this one makes a difference. Maybe I have gotten that one gift in my life that goes beyond the threshold of gifts one can get in a lifetime. Finally arriving at a positive balance so that I may start cherishing more.

So many bad surprises litter this walkway, with few flowers along the road. Counting each blessing, I might have surpassed my lesser judgement and conquered depressing thoughts that plague me from time to time.

Optimism has always been a downfall – for it is tough to get up after falling so far. Slowly having chiseled my mind into something less ethereal, there is a calm now that weighs things with a more even notion.

Hard-to-materialize notions are met with realistic skepticism, for now I know more of how this world works. Pulling the rug out from under myself is a behavior I have learnt from and refrain from doing so vigorously nowadays. Setting myself up to fail seems more difficult.

Going as far as to say I am wiser in my young years is a long stretch, but words do not lend humbleness so easily. Far too simple it is to get one's foot stuck in one's mouth or to think one thought too many. I find the amount of words we use would double if we were more subtle.

Far away from thoughts that dig too deep, today I feel happy in the meantime – somewhere between my dreams and the past, not with immediate deadlines and also not lost in the maelstrom of time. A kind of sweet spot that is praised too highly. Funny how small gifts make such a big difference – yet hoping for them is a spoiler. Through the circumventing of my subject, I paint a bigger picture than it is, yet the things we put into the spotlight shine brighter than the rest.

Life is but a collection of many nothings left to chance coupled with our intent – sometimes the world surprises us when we stop surprising the world with our grand wants and desires. They say happiness is like a butterfly – don't chase, just wait.

Letting Go

Recently I lost hope in myself and the world; I was made aware of how unsafe it is to show what you are. Pushing me to my breaking point, I realized I was holding onto something big inside myself that was skewing who I really was, a construct of wishes and orders to become something I'm not. Just a conglomerate of thoughts that I had been working on, constructed of things I hoped to become and manifest within me, gathered from what I thought the world needed of me.

This 'self' that I constructed was what I think many people build on their entire lives, and it feels fake.

When I speak to someone that is running on one of these constructs it feels as though I'm talking to a mask, a shadow of who they really are. Destroying this construct is a mission of deconstruction – it's like lessening an addiction to fostering this 'being' inside me. My heart is awakening and is dissolving the fake. Having had enough, I feel as though I'm going through a biological battle that has my heart engaged in transmutation in an ongoing cycle of lessening its power over me.

Many deep breaths and assimilations of bravery it takes to continue the siege that is inside me, never giving way to giving in to keeping it there. While this is happening it's like I need to come to terms with the feeling of letting go and just being who I am becoming and who I truly am.

There is a true self that I thought I always was already – a basic form – not who I thought I was. 'Yet, analyzing my spirit,

I find that the basis of me is far simpler than I had anticipated.

It's like going to true basics, and has my life being far simpler than I thought it should be. Cutting out what's too complicated I think is the best form of medicine I can give myself. The overzealous dreams are so complex and it feels as though I'm pouring water into a bucket with a hole in it – putting my faith in something that is not wholly me.

Don't get me wrong – the dreams are great but is it what I really need? It seems I've come to the realization that one's dreams can be this natural thing that seems to be born in – the general purpose of mine, what I know to be my life mission – and then there's world-created dreams that are on top of my actual plan that I would like to achieve for my ego.

It would make me feel better in my mind, but it's just another thing I achieved. It'll boil down to that – that stepping stone I build on among the myriad of stepping stones that form the walkway of my alienation.

It's not like I care enough to use painted-on gold color or anything special – it's merely there to be doing something that people might find to be constructive – so that I can say I'm doing something with my life, even though it does not fulfil me, at least it's something that is socially respected.

Feeling different about myself by doing this task is arduous and it doesn't feel right torturing myself. Before I was torturing myself because I wasn't doing anything and starting was the right decision, but it's like I'm in a play of my own design. Dancing for the crowd that does not care.

This is what I think so many are doing; we aren't true to ourselves anymore, we can't be – making a living requires us to be proficient in some sort of trade and if you happen not to have a trade that makes any money, you are forced to start dancing to a beat, for people that are doing the same that just need someone to take the spotlight.

What I'm getting to is that this façade needs to come down, and we need to align the systems we live in to our true selves so that each one of us can live that out without worry over whether we have food on the table.

We live in abundance that is created for all, but we live under the pressures of having to earn our part through activities that are not spiritually just. Dancing trained monkeys.

This life is just beneath us, or at least me – I am here to learn while I actually live, not here to take part in some competition of who has the best contrived steps. Too many individuals have a foot in the game to make it possible for the average individual to compete. There isn't enough new material in the world to get into the game of who's invented the newest life-benefiting gadget.

It's getting to become disappointment in my fellow man; how can we have spent so much time monkeying around and not have much spiritual good to show for it? When will all the facades break? Life does not have to be amazing all the time – as long as you can be satisfied by being your true self and live peacefully life gets into a groove that feels natural and healthy – how long will it be until we discover that collectively?

The systems we are living in are contorting us into these unnatural beings that seek to contort themselves and each other to stay alive. What a meaningless existence – and this from a 'civilized' culture? Our rules are meant to serve us as well as the systems we work with.

What would be civilized is if we could all live freely and honestly in humbleness and without needing to chase after contentment among other achievements.

It would usher in the era of the heart – where the strength of your heart determines so much more. Respecting peoples heart achievements is healthy, for we are busy praising achievements of the mind and activities of the body. Menial and cold, heartless and soulless. It's so difficult to get into a state in which you can actually work on the spirit and the heart, and it's then looked down upon as if it's a waste of time.

How much I respect those that have worked on themselves. Weak and humble. Rejected by the world and thrust into loneliness – for they are so few. Depressed and self-destructive. Not destroying their whole but always cutting the soul for what they are – true to it.

Life Does Not Have to be Hard

The systems we live by, besides the money system, cannot be spelled out – it's a social discipline that we grow up with and adopt, that then becomes our norm; unnatural and unnecessary. We are forced to conform to notions and arbitrary rituals in a form that is guided by our minds like a belief that has to be maintained. This belief is stimulated all the time in conversation and the actions that go with social interaction. It forms this ghost consciousness that possesses us from within. We seemingly telepathically share our views on this form of distortion, and it keeps controlling us as long as we are unaware of it.

Look at natives; they're doing great with the little they have, and they're looked down upon because they cannot explain to the 'cultured' man what they do differently. When you return to basics life becomes very simple – you take care of what you have and make sure there is enough for the future, but you don't bend over backwards to provide a surplus so that you can be lazy at some point in the future. It's good to work and to have a constant supply of things to do, so why put in the effort now only to squander it with inactivity?

We break ourselves and need to rest deeply – that's why TV is so popular. Spending every ounce of energy on providing us with a lifestyle that is lazy at times is like an addiction to a substance that nearly kills you while you're on it, and as it fades you quickly gather more material to concoct more of it in your disrupted state – doing a bad job of it and creating a less potent derivative.

You want to be at peak performance when making whatever you're working on – this system drains that creative energy to make something a constant. Life does not work that way – one can see it in art; the original works are astounding and as their career progresses the means which they use and the quality of the work increases but that roaring creativity that resounds something new and enticing leaves slowly.

This is because their gift is being abused to produce a consistent result like a machine that does not get enough maintenance. Sometimes it takes years to get proper inspiration after exhausting all the originality in the early works, and then if you have not made enough out of it, you're stifled by the system. Foiled. Unable to regain the balance that gave you so much inspiration to produce those early works.

It's also so difficult to wind the mind into a new view so that one may yield that freshness that the original work had. Your heart's just not in it anymore – the pay cheque is there regardless of quality due to the trust that was built with previous works, and those can always be performed, but to ascend to a new level in one's artistic career, completely reinventing the style, is just too much of a burden.

Working with what you have and displaying yourself should be enough. Everyone should be able to do this and live comfortable lives without question. This is the norm that we can create. The past and our accepted norms bar us along with fear of change and laziness.

There is no excuse for being stagnant, yet what has been built over generations is kept as though it's holy even though it does not serve us. There are so many instances that have become outdated, but their stewards cling to keeping them alive. The collective is almost powerless to stop them in their crusade for keeping their power in place. So much so that oppression is the way of life; in order to stay on the top, one needs to fight off the new and the growing. Cultivate the old with tales of history and propaganda.

Forever rehashing what is to pass, reintroducing it with a tweak into the now as if it were the greatest invention.

The problem I have with it is that it's not like cornflakes with milk that taste good almost every day, or eggs and bacon. It's not a comfortable staple that one can live with – I feel like a prisoner being fed the leftovers of the same meal every night. And all there is to eat is that same meal every day. To the prisoner it's food, because he's close to starving, so he does not notice that that same meal every day is actually making him sick, he just needs the food – but the food's supposed to make his life better in that cell for its all he's got. It is the only new introduction and interaction he has with the outside world – so everything about it makes or breaks him.

Not to promote influence from the outside – his inner life can be grand, but his food is the only significant change he has in his day and so it is with us. We crunch down on the same information every day with so little change in it and once someone with a head start and heart makes it big, we evolve.

This happens so rarely, yet it should be the norm – every day should be one of learning and evolving with the times to produce healthy minds and hearts that engage in sharing of their invigorating lives.

We are not machines. And to boot; even machines need to restart, get maintenance and are not meant to be used 24/7.

Loneliness

Happening on a video about this topic, I noticed I was one of those people that do well with loneliness, but I build up such an number of things that I want to speak about when someone is listening that I can easily overwhelm them with the amount.

So, I write it out and hope that there is someone willing to read my rambling along the lines. Outlets for spiritual people like me are rare in the place I live in, and most people don't have the patience to talk about the subject for such long periods of time.

To me, talking spiritual is almost colloquial in the sense that my mind is wired to take for granted that everyone does spiritual work and can talk about it. So, in this world it seems as though very few like to do spiritual work. Here's someone that nearly only does spiritual work.

I kind of see it as my job to work on our spiritual issues, raising my vibration for the planet so that we all may rise in awareness. Loneliness is a big part of it, so I'm busy finding friends that share the interest so I can replace my internal dialogue with conversation.

There are pitfalls to loneliness like the one I've described, but I don't feel bored with it – there is always a multitude of work to do, so I'm not liable to fall for filling my time with things like being some kind of detrimental part of society. I find these things to be a waste of time along with my lower sides, so I work at my lowest points to raise them up to form a constructive use of time. If I'm going to be alone, I better make the most of it.

You don't need to feel like you're not achieving anything when you're alone; it is very healthy to unwind, and you do not need a TV to do so. We are used to rigid regiments when it comes to relaxation – we always need a beach with some cocktails. Instead, enjoy the calmness of your being, and align with a side of yourself that is more or less content with the quiet.

There is definite virtue to simply analyzing the way you are. It really only comes with time that you start changing things around you. It's a very natural thing to improve your mind or soul's workings as you have traversed some part of it.

Believe me when I say that the world is helped greatly already when you start journeying through your mind, simply curious to see what's in there. So many people can't do that because they're distracted with keeping themselves busy simply so that they don't do that.

It shows that your heart is in a good enough state to let the soul wander. You can be proud of yourself for achieving this step. Our busy lives give us the excuse that we don't have time to do some spiritual work, but that is what keeps a bad cycle going.

It builds up stress and blockages that then need therapy and the inevitable alone time anyway, so giving yourself time in some loneliness is mostly a good thing. Everyone knows reflection is good, but it has this painful aspect to it along with a too-serious or critical trait. Most people are scared of reflection, also, because it will lead themselves to thinking differently, but 'no one's asking you to spontaneously become green or a hippy, of sorts.

Simple mindfulness works wonders for conversation, and peace of mind makes you better at getting your point across. We all love to be listened to, and how can you listen to others when you don't listen to yourself?

All of this can be gained from some loneliness sometimes – so treasure it and don't fall into disconnected behavior that stems from distraction. You might as well get into walking in the garden of your thoughts than fascinated or infatuated with some fad or the latest of the latest.

Material vs. Spiritual

Stumbling upon things in my mind, I came to the impasse of having to overcome the physical and material with spiritual, and mixed up the words as if they were interchangeable. Is it possible that there are people out there that want to overcome the spiritual with material?

This notion seemed laughable at first, and I likened them to flat-earthers in my mind for such a matter defeats itself so easily – they are looking for enlightenment or the spiritual in the physical by achieving a collection of grand sorts or building what cannot be built and so on.

What baffles me the most is that it must be that group that takes the term God, and makes it something we have discovered, and holds the thought up as an idol in their collection.

A friend of mine noted once, in the bible, it says even to not have idols, yet a lot of people idolize God, he thought. To me for a long time it was a being in my mind that grew in presence and grandeur until I destroyed it with all I hated about that delusion. Since then, I refrain from using the word 'God' – for in my mind there should not be a single word that can encompass the endless or infinite, the all that is, the all in all, the 'I am' presence or 'source'.

It's all just an attempt to cage something that is not meant to be caged but aligned to. I don't have all the answers when it comes to this belief, for to me it boils down to what philosophy I can apply in my life that makes it better. Things like working for the greater good and aligning with the 'I am' presence have helped me the most.

I feel like I can do the most for others and myself by aligning to the greater good, and when I sync into or feel the 'I am' presence it calms me down so I can get that done. But it's not such a simple recipe – there is also needing to be who I truly am along with my mood, so there are factors that contribute to a larger picture so that I can function as an individual.

In comparison, I can only imagine a materialistic mind to have God sorted out – he's on my side and he loves me no matter what I do – so they go ahead with chasing after physical riches by their means. It's like a straight-forward, mind-driven robot that has found the answer to being soulless and emotionless.

This philosophical construct has not been confronted with energy, or vibe, or morals – just a factual understanding that things work out physically, the way that is learnt over and over without the vital ingredients.

I jabber on about this while most people don't take it seriously, but if these beings exist, they need dire help, and it would be source of sadness to know how many people think in variants of this way. There is no virtue in chasing after riches if the end result is not somehow enlightenment. The freedom to live out your dreams on a deeper level and experience the heart and mind's wonders make you far richer than any amount of gold or possessions and to boot – if you boil things down, there are no people besides acquaintances in your life that stay there for material gain if you are materialistic. The true joy is having people that care and ones that share emotional journeys as we go through challenging times together.

The construct I outlined was simple, but I think it has done its deed, for it is that flat, superficial and empty consciousness in a nutshell. To be honest, I'm unsure of how to help such people directly, and if I meet someone that is a variant of that I feel pity. For the world even, because there are certainly many that look up to people that have the world so figured out. So, I liken this mental construct to a machine that never stops running. Built to produce and hoard resources that are either used by the living or stashed away with stinginess and a chip on their shoulder.

Meditation

When attempting to focus my energies, I seek to find that space inside me that is in touch with the 'I am' presence. It's like a film of peace where I'm in tune and nothing bothers me – rarely when I do yoga, I get in touch with that presence. The key is not to fall into the 'seeker' state where you don't let it live. It's about opening yourself up to the memory of having gone there and letting go.

There will be many recipes but it's not like a road to a pleasure city, it's more a feeling of aligning to where you're natural. Naturally, it's easier to get there when you've been there before, and you will notice that you have glimpses of this space through many different forms. Philosophy gets me there sometimes, or music. I must say, I'm addicted to getting enlightened through music – that tingling feeling I get along with visions of art depicting enlightenment.

Most of the time it's when my feelings, dreams and intentions align to form that release into that experience of ecstasy. Its transitional, though; know that you can only cherish this in the moment, so treasure it every time!

Keep things fresh and moving forward; don't over listen to music you love, no matter how good it is and don't be shy to turn the volume up! New art is also always good, mostly something that has an emotional connection where you don't need to search too hard for interpretation.

We don't have too much music that's ecstatic in lyrics; I'm

still searching for music where they sing about the joy of life in the average state of being. Celebrating the ordinary – because that's how I feel most of the time – I don't need a reason to be happy.

Meditation keeps that joy alive – I become still often during the day, practicing mindfulness to balance and be healthy. Most of the time you'll be greeted with the mundane everyday thought path at the start, but transmute that into what your goal is. Visual aids like healing hands, cleansing breaths and light are great helpers. Be sure to do this with your intention and knowing that it works if you adhere to it – it's called a practice for a reason, you do something all the time, its active.

It's that, the action is very peaceful and compassionate; self-help. Meditation is the ideal 'do it yourself' health food for your soul, and the more you do it the more natural it feels. The best thing is that you can incorporate it easily just by being still every now and again, so you don't need to become some kind of pro. The knowing that you do that good thing for yourself here and there will make you proud of yourself and will bloom into other great behaviors in your life.

It can flow into your life like water and if you have a compassionate outlook, it will transform it, and if you're busy meditating to cultivate compassion then that's a great start – you will get to a greater sense of self love soon. Through all the brush there is a greater sense of peace ahead!

Mother Earth

Experiencing the life on earth, I have never been much of a fan of the diversity of life on this planet – I have had many dreams where I am off this planet and somewhere else, far more peaceful and aware so that it fits my consciousness. These places are far more real to me than this place – awakened and calm, full of life that is good to itself. The beings on earth live in a struggle for survival, and there is much predation such as in the wilderness. Cutthroat views are rife that gives rise to criminal activity and the goal of making it is nearly solemn..

In my dreams, there is no struggle to survive but more a peaceful aura of living a pure life that is close to a tranquility, that motivates the beings that live in those spaces to live out their truth without the dire need to evolve spontaneously while making a living or plain surviving.

There is a lack of drive to make it, but that is what gives us time to evolve at our own pace and follow the heart without laziness and pressure. It's like you're being cultivated by the planet or the star you live on to 'be', and that's enough. As long as the life on those places is happy and not engaging in some form of distortion or bad behavior, there is absolutely no need for uproar. If there would be any distortion noticed there would be healing ceremonies held to cleanse away the negativity. A sign of how loving the culture there is. I see that kind of behavior as though it's this family that takes care of the wounded immediately because it's the most loving thing one can do.

On earth we are so overwhelmed by so many distortions and misfortunes that we struggle to heal them all – so we are forced bit by bit to do the healing as we go along. Very slowly only are we making progress, for so many souls have incarnated to evolve alongside each other. It's such a very difficult project and it requires so much of us, at times, that we break down into our lower forms and add to the distortion unwillingly.

So, we toil on every day anew, grabbing that hard-earned initiative and courage to make this world that tiny bit better than it was before – feeling like we are but a few enlightening the many that are simply unused to the enlightened life.

It's so passive, the enlightenment, that it goes by so unnoticed that it is almost disregarded as virtuous, but the ones going through the deepest hardship are the way showers to those who idly live every day as though it were just life as they know it. This time I have no great message of hope but knowledge that things will remain ever bettering day by day, and slowly our barriers will be lifted by our oppressors, and they will lessen their plight in such overwhelming control over the culture and become greater seekers of enlightenment. So that, through time, the whole planet's population and the planet itself can align to a better life over the course of the millennium we live in.

It's a testing time, and you will have to swallow the pill that contains the knowledge that progress is slow, because we are so many but for a few there will be leaps in consciousness, and for others there will be pitfalls of lethargic progress. Be that as it may, we will all ascend to higher levels not suddenly but over time. Attempt to adhere to your heart when committing to doing your spiritual work when you feel it would benefit you and others, so that it becomes a joyful thing you can do for everyone without pressure and in your natural state. I cannot stress enough how peaceful a feeling I would love for you to align with, so subtle and almost unnoticed that you may walk in a silky aura of contentment.

Mother earth would love for you to feel at home in your being and know that she is doing the best she can to provide you with a life that is not perfect yet but getting there. You will have to work with her to manifest this desire so that she becomes the radiant planet she is destined to be, with so much wonderful, energetic life on her surface.

Philosophy

At its core, it's like a fountain of youth, because it rejuvenates the spirit continuously without fail the more you work at it. Like building a structure that can always be improved, philosophy takes time, but is worth every step of the way if you're loving what you do!

Like anything, the start is the most difficult, and when you don't see the results immediately it can dampen the mood quite a bit. Having to get up and get things going, not being appreciative and judging too harshly gets you down.

The trick is to engage in the actual doing of the work and not focus too hard on the final result. You might be stuck with good foundations and simply be too tired to work on the walls and all the wonderful cosmetics. Take a breather and let those foundations do their job – soon you will have the energy to continue on.

Foundations are like that – they take a lot of time to get into place and you can be so glad that it's not a house built on sand.

In some cases, people build huts on sand and migrate a lot, ever changing their perspective to what fits best currently. You might be in between, but in the greater sense, you're always building on a temple. You live beyond your earthly existence as the overall soul, and I'm pretty sure your life will go on as a fragment of that. This should not confuse you into thinking you are not an example of the whole in tiny form. Whoever you are at your core you always work on, be it overcoming distraction and the like or refining your talents – it's a continual process that keeps you growing in a direction, whether you're conscious of it or not.

Some choices are automated and some take time to make, so there is the element of free will. In some cases, one feels almost devoid of free will because the responses are so natural and refined, and in other cases one works hard at cultivating a way of being that serves.

The ebbs and flows take you through good and bad times, and it's all within your philosophy that determines how you handle things, and by this, I mean the behaviors and automated responses that you have programmed into yourself.

There are so many things I have learned and have yet to learn, so I'm not yet fluent in handling every blunder I go through, but I've got my foot in the doorway. Most probably I will always have to battle some kind of foe, hopefully merely metaphorical, but I'm very glad it's not one of the foe's I have faced in my past.

So, one goes along tackling distortions and other demons in the metaphysical world and some in the physical, and it's the attitude that determines so much – whether you get up again etc.

Philosophy will be your teacher, always.

Small Man

It's funny how illusions break apart when something you experience weighs on them. Analyzing a relationship in my life and how I've grown up in that certain environment, I always let myself be abused or misunderstood by a stereotype. My kindness is always taken up as weakness and dependency as if I were someone begging for something that I do not really need. I give freely to anyone that asks if I can afford it, yet when I ask for a small favor in return a certain type of person always makes me feel bad for having done so.

When focusing on what they are losing by giving, it's like I'm doing them a disservice and stabbing them in the back on top of it. It is said that the poor are more willing to share and give freely without any want for return, and that is what we thrive on. There are far more poor people in the world that share the wealth that supposedly the rich work for – but that is just the slant that is our money system.

Getting a return on what I give out is not what I aim for, but the little reciprocation I do get I cherish with my heart. Feeling bad for wanting more and holding that belief feels as though that would be seen as arrogant, but those that insist on getting paid their worth are respected for it, and some even play with prices to manipulate that exchange, catapulting individuals into amazing riches that then get squandered in acts of meaningless purchasing of goods that have merely a physical value to them.

So materialistic is our culture that those living at the bottom sustain all the spirit, and those at the top have all the wealth and power. We know that emotion is what we search for, and we appreciate what we get, for we do not see ourselves as these giant forces that pull so much economical weight.

So, life has kept me a small man, not asking for much and giving all I can. In the past, whenever I have dared speaking up or taking a stance, I was bullied down into the place where the powerful liked me voiceless and insecure. Since recently, I have begun working on my self-image and have restored parts of it to a better quality – I am merely a voice among the many, but a voice worth listening to along with the many others. It all depends on taste – since we have abundance, we can tailor ourselves with any color or cloth.

Having lived my style, I have a certain taste that is unique, yet I find that ground rules in this world are materialistically set, and they're difficult to live by. How I wish the system would reflect the spirit of the many – even the beggars on the street that have nothing, would contribute more than some of our richest parts. Whenever I speak to some of them, they're full of belief but their self-image is destroyed. Humanitarian acts are what they abuse to get their next fix, and it is clear to me that they live far more difficult lives than I can imagine. No amount of money will save them, but if we all chose to be without money, we would be left with just pure acts of caring and compassion. It is one of my greatest wishes for this world to go to a resource-based economy, but hardly anyone knows about it and the ones in power venture against it, while the rest does not believe in it or discredits that we can achieve it when regarding the way we're evolving.

The ones in power like to keep the small people small and fight off the ones that rise – if this were not the case, Kennedy would not have been assassinated, we would be chauffeured in electric cars, and our system would work on geothermal power. Our problems are not mechanical – they are spiritual.

Seemingly, we have to outgrow the old system or break it down, and it's far too powerful to break down easily – it will take the entire culture to do that. So, maybe there is a chance, but what I think is more realistic is that we shall outgrow it while breaking down its pillars one by one.

There is much to learn and a great sea to journey over until we can reach our destination. The way there will be enlightening, relieving and tiresome, but we will get there.

Colorful Tactics

Black and white, a world in fight. These have been doing it for years – clear lines and consequences, equally matched in attack and defenses. Dark versus light – only the start is just and right. An ultimate separation of the two, the most basic and plain their colors, through and through. A war will begin that both 'parties accept, the white king to perform his first step.

A gentle but confident first placement is made, silent and almost unnoticed the move from the shade. Testing the waters, a pawn will be brave, careful his footsteps – preventing a close shave. Reinforcements to the point! Strengthen our watch! Intelligence is the key; we'll raise our fortification tonight by a notch!

Swift shifts in the dark, the message suddenly apparent – a burning notion, no time to lament. Forces holding their ground to keep the watchmen safe – blood, sweat, tears and a little faith. One single advantage and the battle is ours – the difference is made here, between minutes and hours.

Information is in, all voices please silent, the messenger; his news might be vibrant. In color, he spoke the enemy queen's frock it must be, that is all I could muster to see. The quarrel is harsh and sacrifices must be made, but do not fear sir; your men, including I, are not afraid! Your war is as much ours as the wives we have waiting at home, with our lives we shall never rest defending your throne!

Coloration on her gown? That would give definite reason to

frown. With food for thought you have provided me, my most thanks I give thee. You are my powers, without you I am none, now set off – back on your run, once again to our men that await your support – you are one of the foundational bricks in our fort.

Her colors – are they as different as mine? So many, and shiny I find. Oh, if they were, my world would be made, together our tones would never fade. This secret I shall keep and reveal only in her presence, into a corner the dark king must creep with fear and reverence. Strategy must be made to decide her keeper, be it the good king or the dark reaper.

Watch towers in the right places and artillery laying wake, knights and footmen ready in wait. Charge their defense's! The loophole makes bare, darkness enlightens with a flare! Slip the queen the message that will make her free, and then assure her the way is open and she must flee. Away from her oppressive husband her path lies, her choice it is – whether he lives or dies.

Without his queen by his side the evil ruler is alone, his servants – loyal and sharp as a knife they are hone. This is a fight not so easily won, by the end of this night one side will triumph, and one will be gone. To the rescue the white king shall appear, shielded behind me you are my dear! One last spell and the demon will be done; nothing left to fear –he'll be overrun.

Words will be our savior and silence will stay, in the black woods of your dismay. The letter she has read and no longer will she hold her tongue, her emotions – too far you had them strung. No longer is she among your allegiance – this she has said. Too many lies she feels she has been fed. Her world is colorful – like mine, in an array of all of it we shall dine. Give up, it's too late – before I am poised to annihilate!

Your actions are feeble and I will have you dead! Your life force will die – empty you will have bled! Servants, attack! Your duty must be done, do it now! In the name of all that's unholy and foul! Pierce their armor, stain the ground red! Their entire hearts – fill them with dread! Do not rest until the deed is over, all our hope rests in the four-leaf clover.

At this moment in time a sound realization, the clover is green; quick, halt the nation! Too late the saving order is given, into his skull a white knight's blade was driven. Possessed, the dark king falls to the ground, the specter escaping, the world now sound. Everyone free to be true to themselves, laughter and joy breaks out, followed by shouts and yells. The kind king and his queen united as one, accompanied by happy folk under the sun.

A merry life for all on the board, good treatment of anyone – that of a lord. No worries about color or hierarchy no more – that is about all we've heard of new lore. Ourselves we can show and our ecstasy you may see, the rest of our lives will be filled with nothing but glee. The white queen is left to find a new mate, she'll be fine – her life will be great.

A burial for the fallen, his thought a bit late – life: a winding road of unchangeable fate. Paths determined by character alone, his unfortunately incorporated being dethroned. Peacefully we would have lived together, one randomly-colored empire on a chess board – forever. King and queen now one of us, in love they will stay, the king with a crush and our wonderful queen – a soft blush.

The Greatest Gift

I realize now that what I wanted to see in the world is what I wanted most dearly for myself. I wished the world would calm down and realize what beauty it had and what answers are already there, waiting to be applied.

No sooner than me having realized that expansion instead of progress is what I needed most did I notice that this aligns with what I wanted the world to experience. So, the next time you find yourself blurting out at the world that it should wake up, calm down, realize the obvious or any other action, give it to yourself. Notice that this is a deep desire within you that you wish to see in the world so that you may see it in yourself.

The trick is that you can give it to yourself first and then see it in the world – for you are the world. The mirror goes on so that you may realize that there are no boundaries. Many things that are in the world can only be changed slowly and with much patience, but you can change yourself much more rapidly.

Most of the time you cannot see beyond a certain fulfilment of a desire or action, so it becomes very difficult to give yourself what you need, but I hope, reading this, you get a shortcut to dissolving negative layers within yourself so that you may take leaps in consciousness.

It is difficult to assess what you truly want from the bottom of your heart, but there is a basic notion that, if fulfilled, will give you peace.

For me there are still desires, but I'm unsure of whether they are as great as my need to have calmed down and continue to do so. I did not know that this great gift was inside me from the start, because I had to fulfil a lifelong search for answers and to finish my dissolution of delusion first before I could receive this gift. It might be similar for you, so this might not be a shortcut but more of a description that you can understand.

The giant quest for answers is more or less soothed in me, and all I have left to do is expand and become harmonious. A sort of sinking into my foundations and relying on them. Easing into my consciousness, I can let go of trivial aspects of mine and center.

As life becomes more effortless, I feel as though I am privileged and that it might be unfair the way I am living spiritually in comparison to others', which make their own lives a sort of hell. It is not my fight, though, and everyone makes their own journey, so I must continue with mine.

The Now Moment

If you haven't entered the now moment yet, it's vital that you do everything in your power to do so. It's where the power lies. I have recently felt as though the world has entered this 'now' moment, and I have been able to let go of so many negative behaviors since this time.

This moment is where I feel at home – it's the literal now that forms an endless moment in which one can introduce what one feels will be a fruitful endeavor. Plans and past memories get sorted so much quicker because there is the focus of taking care of it immediately.

Delving into what the 'now' moment is – it's a mental or soul space that the spirit depends on to live in. Other writers speak of the fifth dimension – the fourth dimension being the dualistic dimension that is the broken timeline that humanity has been sitting in for so much time now.

The fourth dimension is characterized by every positive thought being followed by a negative one, and since the matters are not sorted out immediately, these themes run over the course of your life in fourth dimension. So, in effect, you can be stuck in there your entire life, always planning, hoping, remembering and feeling bad for things that have happened and regretting, along with mourning your life, and the myriad of thoughts you can possibly introduce into your, so to say, filthy now moment.

The fifth dimension, on the other hand, is an open expanse where only what may be fruitful can survive – grudges along with everything that does not serve gets disregarded by the mind as something not worth introducing in this 'living' space. It's like a flower bed with fertile soil, where only relevant topics may be introduced so they can immediately grow into fulfilment.

Getting used to fifth dimension. It's very similar to fourth, with the difference that you can endlessly continue thinking good thoughts that do not trigger bad thoughts or memories of the lower dimension. Over time, you become used to the more jovial feeling of power and ability. It's the natural state for the human – some people say we were built for fifth dimension and it shows on our hands and bodies – our head and four limbs displaying the number five together.

We have been waiting to evolve to fifth dimension forever, for it's been a long time in fourth dimension with so much distortion, war, ego troubles, depressions, illnesses, distraction, disorientation, disconnectedness, delusion and illusion.

With living in fifth dimension in our grasp, we can now take care of all of problems in a fashion that gets immediate results – all the negative results that you may get stem from you, and, getting used to this new dimensional view, you realize that you have the power to pursue your agenda if it is deemed to be introduced into reality.

You also don't get thrown down into fourth dimension so easily, because you are basically prompted with the reconciliation of your misstep to keep you in that higher state of being – always riding the full circle.

The fifth dimension is also where time plays less of a role – eventually you will come to notice that what you intend to do is more rapidly achieved, and later on all technology along with all our system will be adjusted to fit this almost hyper version of immediate satisfaction so that we no longer need to pay later, postpone for later, make plans for later to: longer postpone the rewards –everything needs to be able to be sorted in the 'now'.

I'm not much of a planning guy – I tackle a project head on and attempt to sort it immediately so that I can put my whole heart into it and get the results. It's what I'm used to, and it serves me in a fifth dimensional world, but I'm rather useless in fourth; where it comes to planning out when I want to do things, I have to force myself into action even if I don't feel like it, always having to bend over to the mind so that I can achieve my long-term dreams. It's such a very arduous task, thinking about so many menial details, that I become overwhelmed, and I find it's just not worth the effort. I can't fill my now with so much clutter and then be expected to think at peak performance.

The 'now' moment serves me so much better, and I predict we'll be seeing the world change faster and into something more vital as we go through this year. Introduced hope can actually find ground to grow in and not be disregarded or just marked off as a collective disbelief. We should see that our collective dreams get started, and that life itself will become more vibrant.

It was an exponential curve heading us into this moment, and now that I feel the majority is there, we can start thinking of what we wish to achieve as a collective – the first of which should be to completely get used to living in this moment and shedding the old behaviors that connect us to a distorted world and self-view. Also, celebration is in order.

The Shadow

This is a very important subject, for it is very well known in comparison to other spirit-based topics, and can be dealt with immediately, yielding a sense of pride when having accomplished clearance.

We all have a shadow, and it creeps up on us during our day, always being there to trigger familiar emotions and behaviors. We struggle accessing it and resolving the problems the shadow brings forth because it is usually met with a further pushing down of it, rejection, discreditation or any other form of denial. We don't want to look at it because it's painful, so we postpone work on it for a later date.

It's wonderful, however, feeling as though you are achieving spiritual growth by decreasing the size of your shadow – tiny bit by bit you can release shadow energy by compassionately confronting it with understanding and honesty in mind. It often poses a daunting statement that makes you feel bad and retreat into your emotions – so openly ask the right questions at its edges, slowly sizing it down, so that you can dissolve it day by day until it yields peace and growth.

You will grow comfortable with resolving shadow energies in time and work on them whenever you feel like taking the next step. Some aspects are engrained through years of cultivation, so you might have to work on them for longer periods of time or seek professional help, but step by step you can resolve shadow energy to transform your life. The ones around you will cherish this and you will get up every morning feeling better about yourself.

It has that true sense of working on something, that yields results. Since you can feel the difference by having a calmer mind and heart after releasing shadow energy, you know that it's working. Having spent many a dark day confronting my shadows, I have felt what it's like barking up the wrong tree and hitting walls that just don't collapse. If you do it right, you take down layer for layer until it transmutes into a smooth being that folds into your true self.

As you go along this path you will feel more authentic as you go along – always moving closer to the true you. Of course, there are negative beliefs like *I won't achieve this*, *this is too big* or *I've tried this and it doesn't work*. The shadow is part of yourself that you have not recognized and will get bigger until you give it attention. It's a matter of rethinking the subject in way that has you try to solve the issue with growing perspectives. Facing it head on every time will have it deny you until you stop and take a different approach.

It's you you're dealing with, so treat it in the way that would like to be treated; compassion and honesty once again are vital in decreasing the size of your shadow, and it requires soul exploration.

This means that you will grow as a person when working with your shadow, and to me there are few things that feels as great as personal development!

The Spiral

Starting from a central point, the outward movement always becomes bigger, much like thought – there is an origin that interests and with care or sometimes, involuntary attention it grows to become something greater.

Sooner or later, there is an overflow where things become too much to handle, or a form of revelation is achieved. I let this overflow out in my work – often procrastinating until I can bring something onto paper or canvas.

It's a somewhat torturing experience keeping thoughts in, yet I feel as though I would burden my outside world if I let it out step by step. Regardless of what the best mode of wielding of thought is, we always have unconscious thought that twists in spirals along with the ones we are aware of.

It is a natural and beautiful pattern that shows how things evolve over time.

At times you want situations to spiral, just not out of control. The opposite is also present in a downward spiral where the end is the central point – luckily there is one, for without it we would not get to solutions to complex problems. Naturally, this pattern leads to an answer that is ever closer gotten to – seemingly inescapable.

There is also the notion of hallucination within the spiral, as often used on eyes or above the head when confused or in a trance – it reminds of circumventing a subject to a near fanatical extent and whether we want to or not, there are subjects in our lives that take this form.

The key is to cultivate what serves and to lessen what does not – thoughts naturally spiral because our minds are cyclic – so feeding the good ones and stemming the bad ones is a good practice.

Denial plays a big role in this behavioral cycle, since that which we deny grows on – so do not fill your mind with distraction so that what you are avoiding eventually rises to the surface in frustration or anger.

There are many depictions of our bodies' energies moving in a spiral through us into the outside world, gathering information and returning back to us in a never-ending cycle. We gather from the outside and process to send out, once again, in a continual process.

The spiral can be playful and healing, or it can be something you wish to not fall into; identify with the best aspects of the spiral and you will see the enormous potential the symbol holds for good seeds or how a complex ring will lead to a single answer.

It implies a start or an end, while instilling the reverse, which would be something never ending – yet this is purely theoretical, for there is a start and an end to everything. Mostly the space in between counts.

The Third Eye

Getting some valued stimulus from art I love, I have finally brought myself to writing a piece on the subject that is at the core of my belief.

Being in love with the saying, 'in the land of the blind – the one-eyed man is King,' I find myself no longer so lonely when envisioning or being a man that is so infatuated with the mind and its center. The mystery, this eye holds is depicted, written about and adorned in world culture – the core of mind holds the ability to connect us to all that is, dissolving the barriers we put up and uniting us with the world, regardless of how boundless it is. Through awareness, our minds can only extend to a certain reach, and this eye lets us somehow be 'one' with this entirety. A feeling of connectedness that improves our ability to be compassionate.

Some crave this state, while others let it flow freely into their being by building their lives around entering this divine space as often as possible. I must say that there is no final barrier to getting there, and once you are there it feels so natural that you don't know the difference between before and after having gone 'beyond the veil'.

My vision is blurred due to having experimented with this state all throughout my life, so I no longer know when I am in or out, yet instead I travel between momentarily.

Puncturing, opening and sipping from this space, I seek to spend as much time there as I can to be able to transcend what I find there into the reality of the nearly purely physical.

I say 'nearly' physical,' for I no longer believe that what we seem to know as the physical plane is in fact a film we project collectively and passively. An example would be stone; that which seems very hard and difficult to crack for me, seems like an easy-to-wield substance in a miner's view.

Problems might seem like mountains to some, while others have the solution or some better solutions that make the hurdle be far less difficult.

In my view, the physical plane must be a projection that we have evolutionarily created to 'be' the way it is. A story for another day will be 'higher dimensions', in which the physical might much be capable of being shaped like the spiritual – creatively and with a great understanding of the energy an artist works with.

Getting back to that space that we all want; we seem to be unable to let ourselves create a culture that is in love with this space to the point where we can call it a new normal. We have the building blocks, but they all still need to be chiseled into a masterpiece that may become a new way of living. So much change in perspective still needs to permeate the surface.

A great amount of us are living this enlightened life – moving and self-creating worlds that are shared with the ones that wake up each new day, and helping others wake up to a unified state.

There is, however, a big chunk that is not letting itself experience this kind of greatness, seemingly awkward when put into such a free zone and clinging to cultivated doctrine that determines ways of 'acting' normal yet not being completely comfortable with this state.

The fear-inducing, paranoia-creating and violence-loving side of us is what needs to be dissolved. It seems like the other side of the coin is rooted in such ways of being. Seemingly unable to tear themselves away from the enslavement of the dark forces they are under.

This gives me a sense of having to cure a form of insanity or bring a lasting upheaval to deep-rooted nature that is so engrained that it would take miracles and decades of work to lessen the effect war philosophy and self-justified violence for temporary release from suffering have brought.

There is an air of short sightedness the goes along with being in such deep 'sleep', and I imagine this is what living hell is like.

I have experienced my own version of living hell, yet it is unfathomable to me to think of what I fear other souls are within.

Regardless of how things are – in my sights, I can only comfortably know that everyone wakes up at precisely the right time for them within divine time so that the unnecessary bonds are lifted, and the collective can breathe a breath of fresh air.

I think there have been many in the past that have reached a state pure enlightenment, but found themselves alone. Right now, I feel there is a great movement to more people actively working on these states as a way of being and no longer feeling alone when journeying into such spaces.

It is an opportunity to start an ever-changing growth that sees us working together in a world where we are in harmony with our body's true potential. Biologically, we have this ability to use our mind to their utmost potential, so we should make use of our third eyes – regardless of what negative stigma it has to the individual.

All I can say is that it is truly rewarding, and nothing brings me more reliable peace every day. Spiral out.

Trees of Life

There is so much beauty in the process of things fading. As time goes by, I find myself shedding older perceptions, while reuniting with what was at the same time. A form of growth that makes me feel the change deep within. Pride and maturity yield in lesser quantities, yet thick like honey.

There is a feeling of tapping into a space of the divine, often adorned in meditation, yet a sturdier emotional state. My bedrock is being nourished.

Personal growth is much like having built the stable trunk of a tree and feeling the nutrients move through it to the leaves – addicted to the sun and often forgetting that the basis is sustaining them also.

We dream and hope – producing energy for small and transient, fleeting day to day achievements – so far away from the roots that have greater plans for us.

So, the tree grows in steamroller fashion. Only through realization do we gather how each part of us works in unison.

Each leaf represents life and new beginnings while the branches support. The roots take care and churn to produce a healthy connection. While the tree makes itself a home for other beings, the core holds all of this in place. The air is like a messenger of love and the aura and shade a tree provides is a safe haven.

Gloomy, resilient or magnificent, these wonders of nature and symbology provide serenity in this world, along with release from troubles or comfort in heavier times.

There is an abundant passive kindness in the ones we like to envision and sit under, yet thorn trees still feed the giraffes and antelope that can eat what they bare.

So, I find the spirit to be powerful when in the conquering mode – the right drive, given by the roots and trunk, produces perseverance through hardship. We have no choice but to triumph over difficulty in the end.

Pushing the end point further and further away is natural, but when balance finally rolls itself into being, true grit is proven. Whatever trunk you have been building will either see you weather a storm or let you rebuild and attempt at another time. Cycles of never giving up get stronger and stronger until you will succeed.

Funny how pinnacles become root work so quickly, for lack of reveling in our accomplishments. We connect this too much with ego – a humble acceptance of all that has been done is what we are after, but we all too often fail at grasping the epidemy of our feats due to forgetfulness.

At least this is what I gather today, which I add to the overall tree as an ever-serving entity – so mixed up in my own life and perceptions that I so rarely get to pay tribute.

Yet this feels as though it is my duty – an innate respect I pay on my journey.

Unity

I have recently chosen unity.

There was a space in my mind occupied by dualistic thinking, as if half my brain was on the side of dualism and the other was on the side of unity. Having listened to an audio book by Deepak Chopra, I could get a good picture of what unity consciousness is like, so I aligned with the unity consciousness that was already inside me and let go of the dualism.

I feel less afraid and the shift has brought me to a knowing that there is even more freedom out there! The simplification of the mind creates ease and room for more enjoyment in life. I feel less overwhelmed and know that I can trust in the divine.

As long as I remain in an ever-evolving state of mind that flows with the world, there is no level I cannot achieve. It gives me the utmost joy to benefit society in whatever I do, not neglecting that even when I am negatively influencing the multiverse it is recycled like compost; what I mean is that now in unity it feels as though there is an entire consciousness on my side.

What I do, I do in the interest of the greater good, and I am bent on making myself as productive as I can be – always giving it my heart and soul, while also managing the amount of energy I spend so that I don't give too much.

Being so excited to feel the unity consciousness, I am very eager to contribute more efficiently and need to hold myself back at times, but I have not got enough patience, it seems, to contain my drive for the new.

Associating patience with boredom is one of my faults, but even that is something I can work on that – when removed – will boost the collective that tiny bit more and provide me with even more free flow.

One thing I have realized is that unity consciousness hands you the answer before it hands you difficulties. It might take some getting used to, and small change has to occur that you will be ready for, but only rejecting the answer and looking for a way around the obvious lands you in distortion.

Life makes you ready for the answer when you are ready to receive it. If you look closely, there will have been signs and nuances that point toward the answer permeating your memory. The mind recalls valuable moments and reminds you of them when needed so that you may form a decision based on adequate evidence.

There is a big tie to spirit when it comes to unity consciousness, but falling into it does not leave you alone, instead it has you fall comfortably into a loving embrace where you can feel normal and taken care of.

It's like you've always dreamed it to be – everyone pulling on the same string. Flowing together to celebrate the accomplishments that signify togetherness and individuality alike everyone is engaged in the good of everyone and no-one is left out.

We all matter and everything matters and carries weight. Unity is the best decision I could have made!

View

Every few months I get tired of the way I look at the world – I have to consider that I do not see through the world's eyes and what my perception of the globe is merely my own. Tinkering with my thoughts I do not revamp the entire system, but I conclude that I have, by now, probably overthought into a specific direction.

We get into ruts, and sooner or later things become stale or aggravated – we can only take so much. Nuances change as I progress through weeks of loathing mixed with elation. Strokes of genius litter my months that quickly fade after a piece is done, continually spurring me on to write or paint another one.

It is difficult to really call things the same when the general feeling about similar situations differs. Generalizing is a negative trait and contradicts an optimistic, joyful demeanor. I have a calm and suffering that is in me, yet the joy within me cannot be touched.

Never content sounds negative, but it's a natural behavior to want to move – we achieve daily feats along with monthly milestones and so we are used to circumstances moving in a person-specific and action-deterministic predictable way.

I must be wrong about things, too, so weigh what you read with care for your own opinion.

I shy away from confrontation and strife to lend an eye that is not too controversial as best I can. My opinion does not strike me as being too far-fetched, yet it is gaged by the parameters of what information I take in.

To sum it up: we all have filters that weed out what does not serve – so every point of view needs to be considered as a contribution to the overall. This is where skills like detachment come in. A calm spirit makes better decisions.

This makes me respect Zen teachings along with all other practices that train inner peace. Anger is looked down upon, and points to being out of control.

When I am angry, the reason for being so takes over my entire being and I feel small minded. Becoming the middle point, it is now a problem that needs an immediate solution. My wide mind could use such channeling every now and then, but anger does not feel like it serves me in the greater scheme of things.

It is tiring to think broadly all the time, and even train it to have a more holistic view – but I feel like I wish to encompass everything, understand life, at times. Limited consciousness is a blessing and cultivates humbleness, in the way that you have to learn to be you, regardless of the outside world.

A very tough lesson that we learn throughout our lives – for as we change, so does our world.

Violent Thought

This is what I attribute facts to have the nature of. They seem violent in their nature, for they impose their knowledge with a force that is blatant.

There is a nature of thought that is free and full of love, but also fleeting – for if you repeat them or try to force them in any way, they soon turn black and solid. It reminds of trying to catch a butterfly – sit quietly and appreciate their beauty for that is what you actually want to feel, but try to catch them and then succeed in doing so, you have something dead and physical.

If only every thought in my mind were so full of life as some of them are; I'd be bursting with joy continually. I find that most of my thought has a certainty to it along with comfort and logical confidence. Shaping my mind, I have felt that there were factual thoughts I did impose on my life and that ran some of it. It was terrible to have to slave away at getting rid of such conviction-filled facts, but now my mind's a lot freer.

The key, I'd say, is to shape your mindscape into something that is tailored to your liking. Most people probably sit with having to weed through trained thought or beliefs that have become brittle due to their solidity. It will take so much time to cultivate your mind into something you like, but once it's there, it's an investment that pays off in a massive quality of life improvement. Imagine being happy with how things are going and finding the answers more easily! It's a matter of engaging in the action that will make your mind and heart feel better.

Putting in the effort to satisfy your intuition without bending over backwards.

The practice of sending light into thoughts is relieving and helps a lot because it's the intent of enlightening a knot or disturbance and bringing it into view. This has helped me greatly because it also ties into philosophy and logic. It might seem strange at first, but once you get the hang of it by passively understanding its functionality, it becomes easier to engage in. The thought somehow does not weigh on you that much anymore and loses its solid consistency. Soon you'll want to find thoughts you can shed your light on.

The mind has a feel to it, so, like anything, if you have to drag yourself to fixing it, it will stay that way until your intentions clear and you can imagine with better energy. It's like repairing something physical, but instead of tools you use thought that carries a restorative energy and imagine the betterment one ailment at a time.

It's a long process, and I'm still not in a garden of roses, but my water is running, the grass is green, and the aura is rather tranquil. It's not an amusement park but it fits my style and every person has their own mind space, so yours will have different pictures that you describe it with, or you won't use pictures – it might be emotion or words. Either way – there is a sense that comes to mind when describing it, and that sense changes as you put work in and get passive joy and often active joy through realizations that revitalize, uplift and motivate.

There are many ways that you can work on your mind; some might want to apply visions or dreams and others would just like to cultivate, but know that you need to figure out how to work with your mind and yourself. It will save you a lot of time to take a compassionate approach instead of a *things are going to change!* attitude.

Your thoughts defend themselves with logic and reason, so be prepared to have to transmute with love, kindness, compassion and understanding. Your heart is as much engaged in healing the mind as your mind is, for it is directly affected by what the results of your changes are. Whatever the mind conjures up trickles down into the heart and becomes your reality – so you effectively have the key to sculpting your life one bit at a time. Always for betterment, and if you can do this in terms of the greater good you will be surprised at how quickly you won't recognize that smile in the mirror.

Weapons of Defense

The seemingly conniving act of retreating into oneself to regain power and peace of mind whenever one can is a trick that I often use when faced with dire circumstances in my life.

It has become a self-defense mechanism much like a snail or oyster. Going into my shell to summon some strength before I make my next move is what I am accustomed to, but it's not really a weapon, is it?

A devious and irritating way of communicating I have found is to seemingly find the holes in arguments until the opposing force simply yields from exhaustion. This makes for annoying contact with mentally violent people that like to paint with black. I often feel victimized, offended, misused or insulted when having to deal with such badgering souls that seem to not have calm spirits.

Who do they think they are attacking someone that was on their side at the start of the argument?

We secretly know we're on the same side, we just have to get there together.

The practice and follow through of this knowing is crucial when it comes to arriving at the end all bones intact and feathers merely slightly ruffled.

What also helps is self-determining your dignity as you go. You cannot be sacrificing morals and key stones simply to reach an end that might just be as devastating as the beginning was.

It has to do with outlook and view. What are your primal

goals for conversation on tests? Do you wish to do battle? Do you wish to spread a peaceful feel? Or do you just want to get along for now?

Principles and levels of each version of preferred outcome have a great bearing on your demeanor while exercising your abilities to communicate and govern yourself.

So, this means you have to take the utmost care when taking care of yourself in whatever situation you're in.

I believe this is why mindfulness is such a great strength! For it prepares you to deal with your own perceptions regardless of how tight or loosely a situation is that you might get into.

Baby Steps

When consulting those with success in life – we will be delivered something along the lines of having faith, working hard and believing in your dream. One of your dreams should be your highest self – a being that is good to itself and to the world.

Selfishness hides in the smallest of thoughts and doubts, like, 'I'll never make it so just carry on with what I'm doing for the moment,' and, 'it's too much work for one human to accomplish on their own'. We need to be all we can be, and we know what to do to achieve this – we're just not setting out on the journey that will take us there.

Either procrastinating it or fearing it and the changes it will bring – the challenges we will have to face make us hide in our shells. Taking it one small step at a time is how you do it; set small goals that can be achieved so that they all end up as the road you're travelling on. Envision what your daily plan looks like and don't make things too difficult for yourself – everyone likes to achieve great feats, but make them too great and you'll start skipping out on tasks, getting stressed or even overwhelmed and stop because it's just too much to handle.

We all have a limit of what's possible for us, and pushing that limit is great sometimes but what you're attempting to achieve needs to be realistic.

No one can say how long it takes to actually reach your highest self, but this journey has a great positive and that's that you feel better the longer you're on the road – it gives you satisfaction and gratification every day and makes you stronger and more capable to continue as you go along.

It's truly not just a place you go and then you've been there and done that, crossed off the list, it's a way of being that changes and makes you feel like a traveler meeting new people, learning new things and expanding as you go along your path.

As you get into the groove, you feel like you're moving with the flow of life and you start living in the now instead of the then – put yourself on the path if you're not already on it, and meet some fellow travelers.

Adventure

What adventure is to each of us is different; personally I'm so at peace with my menial existence that adventure for me is engaging in my passions – they provide me with that urge to experience the new and unconquered – I dig deeper into my soul and find new perspectives inside me that I haven't come across, ever developing my perspective to become more rounded and agreeable to others and myself.

    A sense of adventure is vital for things to change in your favor – they provide a necessary escape from what you're used to and feed the body with endorphins and a revitalizing experience.

    Pushing yourself in the natural flow that wants you to achieve more out of your life is a practice that you passively do, and it's so healthy – it's natural growth. You move on once you're ready and take small steps into your adventure – this is far better than organizing your life according to your income or any other external factor. Of course you have to weigh your decisions so that they do not come from a purely selfish place – in effect, balancing yourself continually – to be within the greater good for all. "Everyone wants adventure and I think this is confused with a very temporary dopamine rush. Gambling and drugs are notorious for providing this along with our 'instant gratification' lifestyles. There's something good about a meal you made yourself as opposed to something that you buy and devour as a guilty pleasure – the emotions you go through are completely different. One cherishes the making and the other revels in the mirage of being satisfied by something tasty that costs so little to acquire.

I suppose both examples are examples of adventures, so it seems that it's just dependent on what kind of adventure you're looking for. As long as your adventures don't become all that you live for in some negative way, I'd conclude by saying that as long as there's still adventure in your life, you're fine; if you're missing out then maybe you should do something about it.

Goodness

You deserve the best you can provide for yourself, and it's up to you to call the shots when you feel you're not getting what you deserve. Every person's self-worth deserves to be recognized, and if you do not recognize it few others will. Putting yourself into the shadow of your needs is very self-destructive in the long term – it means that you're settling for less in the meantime, pending on infinity.

You might not be strong enough to fight for yourself yet, but soon the point will come where you will have to stand up against the doubts you have about yourself. Conquering these doubts will slowly but surely have you make life choices that are more gravitational, and might see you moving somewhere new or changing your circle of friends.

I doubt you'll be certain that the change is for the better and that it's what you've been waiting for all your life. It's a giant movement of the heart – that's why it's a safe move. Forgoing what pulls you down and trading it for a world that treasures who you are.

Every day will be slow and steady celebration of your achievements over your lower expectations of yourself and the demons that you've slain.

It might not seem like such a big victory because it's the summation of many tiny steps that have culminated in a new chapter in your life, but that's because it's a natural movement – it feels normal and it's okay to feel good about it.

Goodness is what you're after.

Meaninglessness

Typically, the thought of 'meaningless' occurs after every action you go through that requires little effort – at least that's what the mind spits out when you're aware but bored with what you're doing or searching for meaning.

Now, there are many things wrong with this behavior; for one – being bored is a sign of things not being right inside you. Two – it's an untrue statement that undermines the sense of joy you would feel by realizing that it's not meaningless but a small action in a greater scheme. And three – it's an action you can skip to move on and broaden your mind's scope.

Eat the elephant; there will be many such behaviors inside you once you search and analyze what's going on behind your routines and trains of thoughts. So, by taking the bite, I mean send the thought away and move on, but unlike other thoughts, not caring about this one (which is another technique) is not going to get the job done. You might not notice it, but the emotional action you go through when having this thought still remains even though you might not consciously think 'this is a meaningless action'. The illogical nature it has becomes like an addiction that the body gets used to and repeats without a sound.

Many behaviors of the spirit are like this, and it's up to you to get rid of them to allow the meaning of 'eat the elephant' to become real.

Reality is what we are looking for and one of the questions you may ask yourself is; is this emotionally realistic to feel this way?

Sooner or later, you'll get to a plateau that feels realistic within your own judgement, and I challenge you to find the most realistic perspective when you debate about subjects with your peers – putting yourself into others' shoes and really weighing the opinions of others and your own makes a big difference in your ability to argue a point, and by practicing such interaction you gain confidence. See how long you can debate without getting into a fight or seriously upsetting someone to the point of breaking down the conversation – the longer you hold out, the more fulfilling the process will be and the more you learn passively.

Some people see a debate as a fight and avoid conflict or facing sides of themselves they don't want to share or talk about, and others simply see the argument as invalid and shut down – don't force an issue because this might lead to harm on both sides. Just let it be once you're satisfied with voicing your opinion and substantiating your point of view. If you're not an authority on a subject take a step back and listen – really listening is as much a part of conversation as speaking, even if hearing yourself finally makes the other person shut up, you'll be surprised at how much more smoothly conversations go when you actively listen to who you're talking to.

Exchange becomes a joy and debates become fun and a source of learning.

Sub-conscious

Basically, you fill your subconscious with the sediment of what goes on in your mind – this hide in your lower chakras and is laden with your almost unconscious disappointments and behaviors that then form the way you are.

If you are actively blocking your subconscious, it leads to serious blockages that hinder you freeing yourself for who you truly are, and can lead to serious mental illness.

Cleansing your subconscious is hard work, and you need to be diligent at it – it takes time, which most people 'don't have, so this part of yourself is rarely ever completely clean, but it's what we need to do to move into the beyond. For further along the path lies what we truly seek – an effortless life where everyone plays out their destiny in a giant crescendo.

It's like we walk hand in hand when we ascend – each person opening the door for the other, taking turns with gestures of kindness and compassion.

This kind of celebration of life is sustainable since we have the means and the energy and furthermore the will.

Before, we thought that a kind gesture requires effort and a response, but ascended we know that we do just because it feels good. Paving the way for another to feel that tad better – that showing of affection simply out of the kindness of one's own heart.

Few things feel as great as walking in the love that your heart exudes – like walking on air.

Rational Thought

One thing belief does is take away rational thought – it puts an error into your brain justifying without reason or truth or to put it into the operative word: UNDERSTADING. This way you can think illogically sometimes – without reason. Doesn't that explain the term HOLY WAR quite well?

Or another good one is SPIRITUA L BATTLEFIELD – these terms are antagonistic and confusing. Makes you think 'I thought religion was about peace'.

Well, true peace can be achieved through the prevalence of thinking in terms of the greatest good or at least greater good – this unifies logic among a group of people that determine a plan that is in this interest and then they take course of action as a unit – it's easily determined who's not on board because they'll do something out of the ordinary – outside the greater good. Everyone's mind points the finger at the selfish individual.

Try applying this to a religious group – everyone just does what they want because they believe it's right, i.e. they think it's right or God said it's right and you can't stop me because God or Satan told me, or even Buddha if he does such mischievous things.

The scenario is just not the same – the one is like a puzzle with all the pieces and the other is a bunch of stubborn idiots.

Chaotic.

That's why our world is so distorted – tons of selfish people just doing what they please – everyone sacrificing the other for that dollar. Carnal. Like animals in a survival of the fittest – full of competition, no accurate judgement, no weight on decisions; simply a free for all.

I see that which I always knew clearer now – it's so easy when you explain it in a rational manner.

Self-destruction

When we are young, and as we grow older, sometimes there are habits we adopt that have to do with self-destruction – it's a very common thing, and I'm not talking about the things that come to mind immediately like cigarettes and alcohol but about thoughts we tell ourselves.

We find comfort in being imperfect, so that we have reasons to moan or just think of something that bothers us instead of more pressing issues that are in our faces. Going back to familiar ways of breaking down our own spirit almost is habitual behavior that keeps lurking around every corner – we don't even notice it.

If you're not like this, then count yourself blessed – a heart without any worries is truly a free one – but for the rest of us it's like we're fighting forces of distortion every day, and we win every day when we get rid of one or two.

Only later does one realize that some of them are gone and that one feels better on a passive scale. Exhaling is a natural response the body goes through once you remove a negative behavior, so be prepared to get rid of the tension that will be released from your soul as you become more mindful – especially if you're struggling with depression or a similar mental illness.

Those little lies are a waste of effort, and you want to kick yourself for creating or getting used to them in the first place – now it's a mission to get rid of every one until you feel good enough again.

I don't believe that anyone has no experience with what I've described, but be happy that one day you'll feel free of anything that barres your thought-paths and be able to focus on the people in your life!

Technology

Answers are what we have, but we're not applying them unless there is monetary gain. For instance, back when they developed electricity, there was alternate current and direct current; direct current was almost introduced instead of alternate current because it meant the economy would grow more. If that had occurred, we would have a power station every five kilometers.

In the same way today, we have the Venus project that suggests that we switch over to a resource-based economy that would solve all our problems – no more money, food for the hungry, education for the needy and specialization for the dedicated. But politics and economic growth in this outmoded system bar us from living in this heaven.

Along with no more weapons, we would also get pendulums in our cars that drop like an airbag when the car gets out of control, preventing an accident by stopping the car.

Another marvelous invention is a train that runs around the globe seamlessly, providing free transport to everyone, connecting the world on a greater level; maybe we won't have to spend all our time on our phones to connect anymore.

Furthermore, invention is the life's work of so many. Perfecting a vital piece of machinery changes the way everyone lives together and progresses the culture into new heights. It is extremely beneficial to be thankful for what we have thanks to genius inventions – our lives would not look the same without them.

An expensive improvement would be solar panel streets, and this is something we could have in a resource-based economy. Yet we have to live with what we're used to, and progress that's too fast can be detrimental – we have to outgrow our old ways of life as we move into the new and I think a resource-based economy is something out of sci-fi movies – even though when you look at Singapore it has a certain similarity.

Original Ideas

Many say that there are no more original ideas in the world and I agree to an extent, but regardless of what we do we will still combine new things that lead to something new. They say it's all about what you do with it that matters and this is big because it's so true – how many bands are out there that sound similar, but you choose to listen only to a specific band in a genre?

That individual essence that a specific voice or guitarist or drummer or bassist adds to the band's sound – even better when they all combine beautifully to produce that brilliant music.

Music is just one example – ideas also apply to industry and relationships and many other subjects everywhere in life. There will always be that unique quality that makes something special.

Now, inventors might seriously be focused on something new, but luckily for the rest of us it's our unique qualities that we have that make us something sought after. Honing these qualities should be a big part of your life, because it's like talent that might be wasted if you're trying to be something you just should not be.

Our modern life tries to squeeze us into molds of high performance, but we just aren't that way – we need to shape our professional lives to fit us individually. If you're just struggling to fit your life into place, and you have to cut corners and squash in a little more everywhere, you're breaking your back to make it work – in the long run you'll lose out on the life that you need. Life is a boat of which you are the captain.

Manipulation

This is one of the most feared things we know. The fear of being manipulated and the fear of manipulating others or even yourself, in some cases.

To manipulate one needs an agenda, and it's often within conversation that one does not notice that one has an agenda, or one is frustrated by another person's agenda.

Proving a point is different to an agenda, and is the healthier way to go about navigating a conversation – once you feel you've made your argument valid, the need to continue the conversation decreases and you can freely move on into another direction or end the exchange.

Often, when meeting new people, or finding out more information about an institution, one wonders about their integrity. No-one wants to deal with someone that has ulterior motives, and it becomes a nuisance dealing with these parties – so the relationship suffers.

One is tempted to find closure and have things erupt in a confrontation of intentions to end or solve the problem at hand – something needs to change or it's over.

In these situations, it's vital to find out true motives either by self-realizations or by honest questions about intentions – the answers might not be easy to handle but at least there's change, and, regardless of outcomes, closure on a subject is better than the torture of living with a stake in your heart.

Wounds heal and time apart changes perspectives so that the

relationships can either reignite or become a memory that is learnt from. If intentions are pure then conversations are seamless, but if a party isn't honest, it sows seeds of dissent as seen so often in our media.

The main scenarios that come to mind are global instances that have an ulterior motive as to what they portray, and thereby undermine their audience; the next one that comes to mind is the general motive someone has when it comes to initiating a conversation with a stranger – will the initial icebreaker keep the conversation going or even get a response? Typically, the motives are questioned, and sincerity is tested and judged – this decides whether or not any further actions need to be taken or whether or not there is any merit to a continuation of the exchange. In either scenario there is either a continuation or a breakdown between the ones involved. The less complicated the relationship the less hurt, this is why our lives contain so many emotionless exchanges; simply to make it easier on the heart.

Things are comfortable when you choose what you want and get it, but get something you do not want and then there's trouble. Problems we face cost patience and energy, yet the better one becomes at negotiating with oneself and others the smoother the process toward finding the solution.

Ignorance is a technique used commonly to deal with troubles, but they don't make them go away, so either confront or postpone the confrontation – no matter how you spin it it'll be your attitude that determines the outcome, and a level of understanding the one you're confronting helps a great deal. Compassion is rare but goes a long way when it's sincere.

Size up your capabilities and what you have to offer along with realizing your expectations before you decide to take the next step in resolving a problem – going into a battle hot-headed might make you lose it all together.

Individuality

Going through life, I always wanted to be like the rest because I felt like an outsider, and now I know the truth – I am an outsider. I don't think like everyone else does and I don't do things the way everyone else does; I'm lethargic and go at a very slow pace when it suits me, and go fast when I feel inspired. Some would look at me and see a lazy soul, and from an outside perspective I'd agree, but talk to me one to one and you'll see that I'm interesting if that's your taste.

I feel like I'm some kind of mutation – a being that can't do anything but think, but at least I do that constructively, even though this might be annoying to some I find it to be what I'm built for. I have spoken about living my destiny before and this is it – share my thoughts on topics and make meaningful conversation, maybe produce a game that promotes struggling artists such as myself and all in all somehow get by.

This scheming mischievous rascal getting by; I would have never thought.

I actually see a future for myself, and that's new to me because I thought 'I'd be playing video games in my parents' basement (if they had a basement, that's where I'd stay) until I died of cancer or something like a car crash.

Just a meaningless life that was wasted on trying to convince the globe of my outrageous dreams of heaven on earth.

More has been added to my life and I'm willing to live it to see where it goes. I have missed this perspective – when I was young, I thought like this.

Blue-eyed as ever but more adjusted, and with a calmer mind.

Help

Going about my business, I find that dealing with some people feels like this terrible interrogation of mine – as if they've already judged what I think of them, and slam shut into this mechanical 'thank you' and the rest of the formalities – don't get any closer than the formal talk, and please don't use your emotion on me.

Emotion – when uninterrupted – flows freely, and if a response flows freely both parties gain.

Where are the hopes of that everyday smile? Back when I was an agent, I tried to make everyone's call a blissful one – one where there is a competent employee doing his best to fulfill the wishes of the clients. Some days were better than others; I think I put surprising smiles on some faces and that's what I'm proud of today.

As long as what I write is of benefit to others or myself - I'll continue writing; it's a place where I can live out one of my passions – the sharing of experience and knowledge. Even though I don't find myself to be a specialist in any specific field, I have a knack for tickling or stimulating spiritual growth in myself and others.

No one will come to me specifically to help them with an ascension related query, but where I can poke a bit, I'll definitely have my fun with triggering thinking about some kind of existential perspective.
To rethink what I know about the world works gives me joy – for the brighter your view of existence the happier you are day to day.

It would give me great joy to be able to talk to anyone and have a meaningful conversation just to brighten someone's day, but I've done and tried that, and I've seen others try and not succeed.

Melancholy is underrated and unappreciated, but a sort of given in this world – although, just because you're not jubilant doesn't mean you're not satisfied or living up to your own expectations. I suppose accepting that everyone is on their own path and that I don't need to figure out what that path is gives me satisfaction and eases my constant disappointment at seeing that the world isn't as happy as I'd like it.

There's too much going on in personal lives for me to figure out what each person is going through, and it's a waste of time trying to pry that out of everyone I meet – it's a sort of invasion of privacy I hold off only for the ones dearest to me.

Exercise

Having something jogging the mind is extremely helpful – walking or swimming a bit will do the trick – as long as your mind gets a rest for thinking predominantly. It gives you a breather and lessens stress as well as getting some movement into your body.

Sitting all day can be tiring, and isn't the healthiest of lifestyles, but in this world many of us have no other choice since what we do demands this monotony. Yet there is the occasional break we can take just to freshen up the mind and get things running smoothly again.

Now, regular, harder exercise is good for the body, but there are some of us that would rather lose weight through diet instead of building muscles that become fat some day or another. Not to discredit anyone that likes their physical activity, but if you happen to be more of thinker than the doer, then this chapter is for you.

In order to have a balanced inner life, you need to be real with yourself, and this requires a perspective that is not impeded by a body's inferior state. Eating and drinking healthily is as important as regular movement. Getting the blood going again is very revitalizing and a necessity for a consistent inner perspective.

If you're in a bad mood, you will tend to be harder on yourself and not engage in self-evaluation – it's a bad time to focus inward. Eat something delicious that you made yourself and go for a walk – nothing too stressing. Soon you will be able to go about your daily tasks without getting so frustrated.

Feeling the circulatory system run and being made use of can be as rejuvenating as a realization that brings peace to your soul. Even if that little bit of peace is only a drop in the ocean.

Destiny

I'm sure everyone has a destiny or deeper desire to achieve some great feat. Fulfilling my destiny is what makes me happy, and even though I'm not rolling in my riches, I get by having a life without worries that are deeper than what I can handle. It feels as though I'm on the right path while it's also not the easiest path. I don't have major regrets and walking it comes easily, even if it takes the patience out of me sometimes.

I'm not intent on arriving somewhere specific in a set amount of time, and the view is great – I don't get overly tired of what I'm doing, and I don't want a change of profession. Winning the lotto or a getaway is also not one of my greatest interests – reaching more people and making a bigger difference is, though. I think living your destiny is like living a dream that expands and pushes your limits as you go about walking/roaming, syncing with the general challenges life throws at you, wanting you to take the next steps.

If you happen to have gotten off your destiny's path, I don't know how you're surviving spiritually, but I can tell you this: all roads lead to Rome. It's been displayed in so many stories that no matter what you do, you're always somehow on your destiny's path.

Another quote I like is, 'I took the road less traveled and it has made all the difference'. Now, this might not be true for everyone, or maybe everyone feels as though they're on the road less traveled because each person's path is different and unique –

I hope it's the latter. Either way, aligning with your destiny might not land you in Eden, but it will make your journey worth the while – you will feel like you have time to look around instead of just wanting to get to a destination and then repeat some other menial process, in search of the next menial process that can occupy your mind while you postpone the spiritual.

Wake up and smell the roses, if you may.

Depression

What we deal with on some level every day, whether it's the global climate or just our lives state – we all know depression all too well. Whether or not this is overwhelming or not determines whether we suffer from a true case of paralyzing depression. I always have that feeling in my soul that something's not right and it weighs on my emotions – some days more than others. Doing something about it every day gives me strength and hope that my future is better continually.

From experience, I can say that my case is no longer treatment-necessary, and I now still feel it, but it seems to have become a general fear about our global future – not knowing what will happen, the state of the country I live in, and general global issues. It has been something that I find commonly in our culture. I hear many complaints about things that I also find unacceptable, and I know that the solutions breach the scope of the individual.

This world has issues that we can only commonly overcome, and some fear that pressures more than others.

Sensitive individuals are more prone to depression than the ones that can deal with a lot of stress, so it's only natural that some of us feel the weight of the world or our lives more than others, and I think that it's these sensitives that will change the face of our collective future.

By listening to their feedback, we will become more compassionate, listen more and solve our spiritual crisis. Our problems stashed away will become physical boundaries that we will have to overcome if we want to be a global culture that can actually have some dignity.

A sort of patriotism that makes you a citizen of the world instead of resident in a country that is run like a business; cold-hearted and methodical.

Achieving

I have sat and thought long and hard about what's blocking me from realizing my true potential, and I've noticed that there were things I thought were sorted inside me that kept coming up.

My initiative is high when it comes to dealing with small bites I need to take out of the feast that lays before me when it comes to spirituality – I can sit for hours beating around the bush, ignoring that feeling my soul spits out every time I go near it.

A secret un-truth about me that I keep sorting over and over again, never truly confronting it head on, and, the truth is, I don't know how to confront it this way. It's not like I can face it realistically like I would a person and tell them what I feel is the reality of things; it keeps nipping at my heels, always being sidetracked with a version of the truth, all because what it claims is blatantly untrue about me, so I disregard its seriousness.

It's come to the point where I simply can't live with it any more, and something needs to be done.

"So, I am attempting to more serious and without the attitude of dealing with someone in wrong in the manner of condescension even when I find they do not deserve my full attention or respect, regardless of how unjustified the claims are.

It's an aspect of me I'm talking to, and as long as it's an aspect I'm attempting to sort out, it's a broken part of me I'm ignoring.

The problem is that it's annoying and it won't go away without a fight, and I've been fostering it for many years, so getting rid of it is going to be work for me.

It's rewiring my brain, conscience and heart to no longer engage in detrimental behavior, but instead skip the step or bridge it in a manner that is healthy, replacing the lost time with spirit-building behavior such as gratitude or peace of mind.

I think I am not the only one with similar difficulty – spirituality is the same in the sense that you get small benefits every time you work at it, but the results are not felt or seen immediately; it's a long road of thinking and contemplating and thinking and contemplating over and over again, constantly self-reflecting, loosening insecurities and feeling helpless or without answers.

No-one wants to willingly subject themselves to their judging minds, and always have to work at updating their self-image – I suspect it's easier to achieve some great feat and live off of the attention and praise that one gets from the achievement; have the outside gratify the inside so that you don't have to do it yourself.

But it's this willingness to finish something big, enormous and daunting to yourself that's the challenge. We can do it, but we choose to do it half-heartedly; if it's not easy then there's something wrong; it's unnatural, because we're used to things being made easy for us.

The truth is, it's difficult to start, but training and morphing oneself into a being that takes care of its weaknesses, making them strengths, is a greater being than you were before.

So, take the step, take the swing, take the bite, just go all in – as a perfect circle song would go. We can do it.

Analysis Paralysis

When thinking continually, you may hit a wall of thought that circles around and repeats itself in different forms. It's often best to take a step back and perceive from a higher or further perspective; do things that require focus on them and take away the focus on whatever block you may have. Do not pursue the issue like you're hounding it down – this will only make you frustrated, and sooner or later you'll start complaining and feeling powerless.

A fresh perspective on an issue is often gained through sleep, as your mind gets used to the idea and find peace or solutions to the problem.

Another trick would be to never get into the state of analysis-paralysis by getting used to in reducing new viewpoints to your internal argument. Think of what other parties might think – there is an abundance of examples I can give, the first one being the nature enthusiast opposed to a capitalist or trust-fund baby. Family members are also a good example, or just your peers would be a logical choice. Putting yourself into the shoes of others is a very handy technique and it builds a balanced view of the world along with boosting your compassion and ability to accept others for who they are.

In the end, there's so much you can think about, that if you hit a wall on a subject, you can move on to the last thing that you liked thinking about – the world has many issues that need creative minds solving these problems and every bit of progress is shared passively with the entire globe and the all that is.

Many believe we live in a matrix where each of us is an expression of the whole – this pattern is found in nature where it doesn't matter how far you zoom into a leaf you will find its basic shape even among its smallest cells. In the same way, we are endless beings encompassed in a physical form. This means you can speak to the universe, and it listens, and furthermore it means all your progress isn't wasted just on you, but your evolution evolves and motivates those around you and everyone else, really.

This means we are all playing a role in awakening the entire species, and also means a great deal for your karma; by helping others, your karma grows, so you could be doing the best for yourself and the ones you affect by working on your spirit and then passively helping others evolve, too. Win

Judgement

Reacting to a statement often is the natural impulse one goes through, and this happens many times a day, especially when you suffer from insecurity or you're very unbalanced. Stress also triggers outbursts or irritation just get the better of you.

When disagreements appear, calming down is needed to regain composure and this happens internally also. Often when doing spiritual work, you will disagree with your own opinion on certain issues – your need for perfection or at least a better view of the same situation leads to more thought on the subject. It's an ongoing battle for the best way to handle the subject; often being as humble as possible is the way to go, admitting faults and forgiving yourself.

Compromise is vital when there are no more arguments to present or other perspectives to be considered.

When it comes to what others think, it's mostly useless to wonder, since you can't change what you suspect they think except by showing your true colors or discarding them. This is where being able to understand their point of view plays a big role, and if you can't figure that out then what's the point? You're breaking your back on a hunch or simply something you yourself dreamed up and are reacting to it as if it we're real – this behavior is you being out of control, and it's a terrible feeling being so helpless, but nonetheless it happens all the time.

Finding out later when you've gathered more information on the subject is wiser and puts the leverage back in your favor –

until then you're just wondering and suspecting.

Premature judgement leads to illusion as well as judgement with inadequate facts. Small delusions plague our lives, so it's easier to have a balanced perspective that knows what it's dealing with instead of sharing without concrete proof of opinion.

At least add humbling words when you're speaking from little experience or in concrete evidence – it softens the blow when you're proven wrong or there simply isn't an explanation. One can't walk around expecting everyone to have the same opinion you do, but realizations speak volumes.

A realization is the biological product of truths that have added up and yielded a conclusion, so it's a safe bet sharing realization, because you can back them but copying something and passing it on as your own is untruthful and shallow.

Just because you've read it somewhere doesn't mean it's true – questioning validity is vital to our daily survival because, at the end of the day, you have to live with your own opinion, and if that's fake then who can you trust?

Listening

This is probably one of the most important tasks you can do - when listening to your inner thoughts what your heart goes through and to your loved ones or just the people you're talking to. It makes you open to input, because you open yourself up to taking the full information in and prepare yourself for your response.

Do not confuse this for just waiting until you can speak, but really take in what is said to you and you'll notice the emotions your conversation partner goes through to have you deliver an appropriate response – not just what you've made up your mind to say half way through.

It's not a test to which you know the answer – that's interpreting you know what the other person is thinking, or trying to make them shut up by talking over them. Let them have their say and you'll get used to having yours – patience is truly a virtue when it comes to listening.

Most people don't have anyone that really listens to them. You feel when a person cares, or has other thoughts in their head, is uninterested or distracted.

I struggled for a long time before I found a few people that listen to what I had to say – mostly I got lost in the endless sea of people that knew the answer,' or had their mind made up already. So, there's really very little room to play with. It gets lost in our busy world – choosing work over connection. We struggle with it and, in my opinion, it must be stress related.

That feeling of being dealt with creeps up, and you feel used or manipulated like it's a job on its own listening to you. Here it's of high value to find the ones that care about you and that enjoy sharing their time with you.

Getting that feeling of your opinion being appreciated is what you're after, not like a carrot at the end of a stick but the true feeling. To some people its common and undervalued, and to people like me it's rare and treasured more than gold.

According to my temperament, I'm drawn to verbal connection and express my love through sharing, so it was very detrimental to my soul being rejected for my convictions and general ulterior viewpoint in the society I was spiraling within. I have since changed my friends and in general the people I have contact to – it's not been easy, but life is better when you're understood and surrounded by like-minded people.

Sharing is caring.

Music

Learning to influence your states using music is a vital skill – I mostly use music to get enlightened. I happens when I listen to something I love and find brilliant; my entire body wants move with the beat and I feel a tingle go through my mind down my neck and into my spine and arms. Sometimes I have a full body enlightenment; it's like when I started meditating. Soon, though, I lost my 'high' that I got from meditation and went into a state of constant mindfulness; nowadays when I do meditate I do it lying down instead of sitting like the masters do. I've kind of lost the patience because I feel like I'm there all the time. It also has to do with my heart – using what I feel as a compass, I know where to go in my mind.

Sometimes I push myself, but most of it's done through convincing myself it's the best course of action, and so in the higher interest that is the greater good, so I agree and go ahead.

The music you listen to affects your entire brain and when you're really enjoying it you dance, as I'm sure you know. The point I'm making, is that it's a natural chain reaction – it's not like deciding you're going to dance at a club because its now time to dance.

The more you feel the music, the better, so really look for that stimulating sound. I would definitely advise you to get some sort of streaming service; they're usually cheap and give you the world.

If you're attempting to push the limits, listen to music that has stimulating lyrics so that you can relate on a spiritual level so it all sync's up.

I could give you a list of names, but I prefer to let you listen with your heart and soul to what makes you feel alive and real. Music is all about integrating your entire being, and therefore a big part of our culture, even though it's been dragged through the mud by night clubs with bad taste that you have to dance to; taste has also slumped into a hole.

You can become a real professional in listening to music of your taste- there are many brilliant artists out there, and it shouldn't take you long to find the ones that stand out because they stick out a mile if you listen. There's the mainstream and the elevator music, then there are the copies, and then eventually you get to the individuals that just make it all come together for you.

Enjoy yourself – it's like food for your soul.

Projection

Reflecting, I have noticed that exactly what annoyed me about my outer world is what seemed to be wrong inside – truly as without so within.

I feel as though I'm wandering in delusion, not having someone to blame or criticize, someone that has a problem I can find a solution for.

The outside signs of disconnection were a reflection of my own disconnection to myself – I don't feel as judgmental as before, simply accepting more that everyone is struggling with their demons in the same way I am, doing their best at the pace they're used to. So regardless of how long it might take, I'm trusting the feeling more than the time now. Instead of setting some kind of time limit, I'm just focusing on my emotional state.

One's heart is constantly being blocked by what I like to just name 'distortion'. The mind convinces itself that its conclusions are the way forward, and send the appropriate impulse to the heart which then gets a minor attack or free flows.

I suppose the 'agenda' is to gain complete free flow of the heart. I say agenda because that's what the mind likes compiling; some kind of plan or course of action that leads to a result.

We're trained to think this way, but dislike talking to people that clearly have a blatant agenda, somehow talking into infinity until they get what they want – a true heart does not do this.

I'm not sure how my future will look, but I am making an active effort to no longer project my flaws into the emptiness of an open conversation. I attempt to be honest with myself and others so that at least that force to respond on what I project as a response is removed, leaving others to freely express what they feel in return.

Giving freedom to others is a gift that I have neglected and want to rediscover anew.

Fear

Being scared of something gives it power over you – you flee from it, and it chases. We spend a long time either running from what we fear, or trying to figure out what kind of fear is blocking our path to progress.

Confronting your darkness is something that you need to do regularly, and you never know what might be lurking in your subconscious. So, take your time and sort your fears out one by one – you will feel closer to your true self as you vanquish them.

Getting closer to your true self makes you freer in your being and opens you up to more self-expression; you might even start taking risks again and not regretting it.

A safe life is what our lives eventually boil down to, and menial attitudes and behaviors get the best of us, but it's vital to take up challenges and complete tasks that you set out to do.

Talking about your fears without wanting to get rid of them is one of the blocks many people face – kind of like adopting a disability. Nevertheless, talking about them is a step in the right direction – it makes you more conscious of how you feel about the subject, and there is no more powerful fear dispeller than your heart.

Your heart resonates a frequency that does a great deal of healing or harm, so be mindful of what trickles down from your head into your heart. It's like growing thoughts in your mind that take root in your heart and soul, and what we are attempting to change is your state of being – cleaning the soul of pollutants we feed ourselves through various means.

Attempt to stay away from 'trying' as it isn't 'doing'. You go through a different process when trying than when doing, so practice replacing these words in your thought paths.

Fear takes away our ability to act upon a scenario, and replaces it with a negative reaction. Really work at culling the angst, and fill your being with a positive action, like understanding.

Dig for the reasons you're scared, and circle the fear until it leaves – it might take some conscious awareness that might be stressful, but life with less fear is far brighter than constantly hunting yourself down for reasons you already know.

Numb

I have felt this way most of my life – just pain, all the time. I was in deep delusion, and I knew it, but I was fighting it all the way. I knew my true self would find a way and now there's nothing left – I slew my demons one at a time, every day, and I'm sure you're tired of hearing about my life, but that's what I had to do, and that's what it takes to get rid of what ails you.

It's a ton of diligent sorting and reflecting, so I advise that you check into your parents' basement for a while. In times long ago, people used to stray into the wild on end which I find similar to an ayahuasca trip—really getting that time to sort yourself out. If you're in any kind of delusion like I was in, then you know you need it – if you're numb, get help.

It's difficult to admit to yourself that you need it or to ask for help from others, because no-one can look into your mind and see for themselves – it's more of a feeling that's different with everyone. I find people that are crazy, in my opinion, every day, and I've met some real nutters, extremists and just downright confused people. It's too easy to classify someone as crazy if you don't have an understanding of that person, and I think that's really missing in modern medicine practice. If it were me classifying me, I'd say I was confused and am better now, just with a passion for philosophy and a general dislike of religion.

I feel like I was a book judged by its cover and hearsay, and if that's you then make the ones treating you aware, but don't struggle too much – convictions can be strong.

It's the fear of classification that gets you – judgement and you're off to the loony bin. I got more ill from the places I went to because I couldn't go home where the acceptance was – only after I got classified did I receive that love again, along with treatment.

They say self-treatment might make you worse, but it's a mental illness. Who can fix you but you? You have to do the work. If this is all too overwhelming for you, put the book down and try again tomorrow or whenever – the last thing I want to do is scare you or trigger some kind of negative reaction; even mentioning it makes me feel bad. I know how fragile you feel and how soft your heart is. It's going to take some effort to heal you, but you'll get there to spite the negativity and the declarations.

We're all afraid sometimes, but we have to be brave – not only for ourselves but for the ones that care about us. Most of the time they're more afraid than you are; it's easy being confused – you're used to it, but others just suspect and don't pry.

Talk to someone safe about what you're going through regularly so that there is trust. I was petrified of routine because I knew I had to listen to my heart, but I got placed into one and secretly didn't adhere to it. It made all the difference. If people are wrong about you, and it's in your heart that you know how to treat what bothers you, then do it, but discuss your actions or plans with someone.

I've met people that are suicide risks and that cut themselves, and in these cases it's wise to have heart to hearts. If that's too much pressure, have that heart to heart with yourself and don't focus on what your mind thinks too much. Focus on your true wants and desires – if death is really the answer, you would have made up your mind long ago and planned it. It's like a ritual you go through. Self-sacrifice for the self.

Integration

Learning to give yourself time to absorb what you have discovered is a task on its own. You might be doing a lot of yoga, or meditating or just thinking about your life and its place in the multiverse a lot, so make a conscious effort to work through and assimilate what you have come across.

There will always be a phase where the new becomes accepted as the norm. I experience this with working through an audio book that has me thinking about the mentioned concepts and information a long time after I listen to a chapter – sometimes I feel so full of new information that I stop the playback to finish a chapter another time.

If you have reached a good basis, it's easier to recognize when you are full, much of the time we spend unlocking new truths, and finding answers but can't get enough, so we go on without integration. Other times we can get stuck and need to transmute heavy energy that also takes time; some truths that serve as building blocks for transmutation need to become conscious tools that you can then use to transmute faster and more efficiently.

Often, I find that I must stay with the process and not forget the tail of the train of thought while building healthy attitudes toward healing the problem. Having gotten stuck in loops and uncertainties, this is an arduous process that can have you trapped often, but keep at it. Try to not lose sight of the overall goal and apply a variant of solutions of more emphasis on your points.

This is typically what many people would describe as an

insane person arguing with his mind, and it often reminds me of such, but it has worked. Even though I don't feel normal analyzing and confronting my convictions in various different styles, I have gone through transformation from someone that was very mentally complicated and confused to someone that is very happy with his mind-state.

Still having the repercussions of such intense thought-path analysis and reforging, I think of myself as a survivor of what would have been my life ending prematurely in some act of attracting an illness, accident or suicide.

This is the type of thing that creeps up on you while you're not giving your spirit the attention it needs. Other things become more interesting, and soon the distraction of suicide, for instance, becomes the weak way out.

You will always work on yourself regardless of whether you have to or whether it's just a nice activity. So, making matters worse is not in your best interest. A key is to align with your greater good, or if you want to put pressure on yourself – the greatest good there is. If you commit to doing things in these terms you are putting in a cornerstone to your betterment and once aligned, all you're doing will flow naturally along this path.

It takes some convincing, though, because you might have to work through some rubble to get you to adhere to this path. Overall, though, it's truly a wonder to know that whatever comes your way is somehow connected to this greatest good.

So, if you need to unwind, give yourself a break and get into the integration mood as you remember the nice things you've come across and smile at how they're now a part of you instead of something you want to live up to.

So, you will grow on, always building on your temple. Remember, thoughts are things, so it comes as no surprise that it really feels like you're adding to something that will benefit you eternally.

Afterword

Having torn through what I have thought about the last couple of years (~2015-2021), I hope that you have found a sense of contentment within yourself as I have.

Writing has given me an area where I can express my deepest thoughts, that I cannot seem to get to as often as I wish to. So, if you benefited from my sharing, I sincerely thank you!

Be sure that I will not stop writing my thoughts down in the most creative way I can so that it might be pleasing to the mind of the reader.

I appreciate the process all the way from difficult-to-reach-realizations to happy-go-lucky, playful contemplation within the borders of my consciousness.

As always, there is more to discover, and I wish to have your audience in my future 'peaces'! So, I bid you farewell, and may the force of balance in all forms be with you!

– F.C. Jensen